Hurricane Lucy

A CAREGIVER'S GUIDE
NAVIGATING THE STORM OF
CARING FOR YOUR AGING PARENT

Always remember to put your own oxygen mask on first! :)

Praise for **Hurricane Lucy** A CAREGIVER'S GUIDE

Navigating the Storm of Caring for Your Aging Parent

"After surviving as a caregiver for both of my elderly parents, I can only say I wish the book *Hurricane Lucy* had been available seven years ago. By sharing her heartwarming story and experience, Elaine Lombardi takes you to a place that no one wants to talk about, yet we are either living it every day or will someday. If you are a caregiver now, or have aging parents, I highly recommend you read this book. The valuable tips and strategies offered in the Caregiver's Guide section will keep you healthy, thriving, and may even save *your* life."   KIM ROBINSON NETO, CHHC
Author of Stop Surviving, Start Thriving
Find Your Perfect Balance in a Not-So-Perfect World

"Elaine Lombardi's *Hurricane Lucy* is a roadmap for caregivers. She shares how to control the storm by sharing with you stories, tips, self-care and recipes so you have energy for your loved one and are able to give them dignity and enhance their health and spirit. I found it very valuable in helping with my MIL with Alzheimer's who lives with us."

LISARENEE CIANCIO-FOGARTY
Author of NO Permission Needed
Ending the Cycle of Verbal Abuse

"Hurricane Lucy" embodies a touching memoir from a daughter who accepted the role of caregiver to her aging mother and a practical guide to self-care for those who take on this role. The book provides insights throughout for caregivers at every stage of the hurricane and emerge with a deeper love and appreciation for the evolved relationship with their parent."   ANDREW LOMBARDI
Author of WebSocket
Speaker, Web Developer
www.AndrewLombardi.com
www.mysticcoders.com

"I had the privilege of reading Elaine Lombardi's manuscript for her up and coming book, "Hurricane Lucy." Lombardi's book is well written, informative and entertaining - I'd love to see it on the silver screen!"

PEGGY EDWARDS
Author of Alfabeto Crossover Alphabet and Lalalandia

"I watched Elaine care for her mother for years. I saw it take a toll on her and how she was able to turn it all around. This book is so informative with so many helpful tips and recipes, along with the real story of what happens, while caring for a parent." KRISTINA FAITH
Preschool Director and Teacher
www.BusyLittlePreschoolers.com
www.AnotherBusyMom.com

"Elaine has written a very interesting and easy to read book that is informative and comes right from her heart. It is full of terrific tips that will help full time caregivers deal with stress, nourish themselves and find joy in their life as they are caring for their loved ones. This book is a much needed gem!" CATHY ORMON, CHC
Author of The Sugar Switch:
The Powerful Key to Lose Weight, Look Good and Feel Great!
Increasing Energy without Dieting

"If you are finding yourself in the position of taking care of an elderly parent, then you must read this book! Not only is this book about a families' struggles, it gives you great information and guidance on ways to make life a little easier. Elaine drew me into her life, every step of the way, feeling every emotion. This book is not just a guide for caregivers, but a lesson for us all." CHERYL DUCAT WIEDENFELD, CHHC
Author of Are You Running With Your Hair On Fire?

"I have close family members who will soon be dealing with aging parents. The insights and tips provided in this book will certainly be helpful to them and others in similar situations." ANN MARIE LASTRAPES

Hurricane Lucy

A CAREGIVER'S GUIDE
NAVIGATING THE STORM OF
CARING FOR YOUR AGING PARENT

Elaine Lombardi

MEL BOOKS
LAGUNA WOODS, CALIFORNIA

ISBN 9780986128707
FIRST EDITION, 2015

Cover Design by Daniel Lombardi
Author Photographer © Daniel Lombardi
Book Layout by MEL BOOKS

The content of this book is for general instruction only. Each person's physical, emotional, and spiritual condition is unique. The instruction in this book is not intended to replace or interrupt the reader's relationship with a physician or other professional. Please consult your doctor for matters pertaining to your specific health and diet.

Library of Congress Cataloging-in-Publication Data
Library of Congress Control Number: 2015905539
MEL BOOKS, LAGUNA WOODS, CALIFORNIA

Lombardi, Elaine
HURRICANE LUCY: A CAREGIVERS GUIDE navigating the storm of caring for your aging parent / Elaine Lombardi. —1st ed.
ISBN-10: 0986128708
ISBN-13: 978-0-9861287-0-7 (trade pbk. : alk paper) 1. Caregiver   2. Self Help
3. Elder Care   4. Health   5. Aging   6. Wellness   I. Lombardi, Elaine   II.Title

Printed in the United States of America

Contents

"Everybody Loves Grandma Lucy."

Dedicated to the memory of my mother Lucille Perrin.
Mom, you've made me laugh, made me cry,
wiped my tears, hugged me tight, watched me succeed,
seen me fail, cheered me on, kept me going
and drove me crazy for the past sixty-three years.
I love you for all you've taught me
as a child, an adult and caregiver.

"The miracle of gratitude is that it shifts your perception to such an extent that it changes the world we see."

~ Dr. Robert Holden

Acknowledgments

Love and a heartfelt thank you to my dear husband Michael, for all
your steadfast support. I appreciate the compassion
you have shown my mother all these years.
I couldn't have weathered the storm of our lives without you.

I'd like to acknowledge our children, my shining star,
my sunbeam, my moonchild and my lucky clover.
You are the precious jewels in the treasure chest of my life,
and you brought pure joy to your Grandma Lucy.

Love and admiration to the amazingly talented, generous,
gutsy woman that you are, Kristina Faith. You held me up when I
was on the verge of falling down so many times. You lent me your
shoulder to cry on during my darkest days and lifted my spirits to
brighten my day with laughter when I needed it most.
Thank you for always encouraging me to follow my dreams.

Thank you John Faith, for your loyalty and tolerance,
your helping hand and your amazing patience.

Joseph Lombardi, thank you for being my rock.
I always knew I could count on you for anything.
You have been there for me in the
kindest of ways with loving help and support.

Jihee Kang Lombardi, I am so grateful to you for
all your hugs and the words of loving encouragement
that you have shared with me.

Bob Perrin I love you more than you know and sincerely appreciate
and thank you for the lessons only you could teach me.

I'd also like to acknowledge the relatives on
my mother's side of the family, especially
Eleanor and Patricia Intiso,
and Lorena, Amanda, and Jennifer Depaz
for the love, help, encouragement and support
you have all shown me throughout the journey
we were all on together with my mother.

Special thanks and much appreciation to
Theresa S. Valenzuela for your editing expertise,
for sharing your wisdom with me throughout the years and
for the insights you have shared in the Foreword for this book.

Andrew Lombardi I am forever grateful to you
for the strength and encouragement that
you have always sent my way.

Thank you Daniel Lombardi for your amazing talent
in designing the perfect cover for the sentiments and the statements
of Hurricane Lucy that I wanted the cover of this book to capture.

Thank you Joshua Rosenthal and Lindsey Smith
for all your help, guidance and support during the
writing process and the extra push I needed to make
my book become a reality. I am grateful to you both
for encouraging me to write from my heart.
It has been an honor to share my authentic self with you.

I'd also like to say a very special thank you to Cathy Ormon for the
last minute edits that you did. It is much appreciated my friend.

Kathy, Jane, Ann Marie, Clara, Liz, Leslie, Vicki and Farrah
Thank you all for being such patient and understanding friends.

HOW TO GET THE MOST FROM THIS BOOK

There are books written to address old age, Dementia and Alzheimer's diseases. Countless websites list agencies to support the elderly. At your local senior center you'll find pamphlets advertising assisted living facilities for your loved one. This book is not about that. Instead, this book is a self-care guide written for you, the primary caregiver to your aging parent.

Although everyone's family is different and every situation is unique, within Elaine's story there are common threads that run through the lessons to be learned as you read this book. Help tips accompany each of the chapters within her story. This book also contains **THE CAREGIVER'S GUIDE** where she shares many of the techniques she uses in her signature H.E.A.L. Approach program.

THERE ARE 3 WAYS TO READ THIS BOOK:

1. Intrigued by the memoir aspect of the story? Read it through and sideline the self-help portions of the book to read a heartfelt account of a beautiful mother and daughter bond.

2. Interested in the self-help aspect of the book and the self-care sections? Flip through the memoir portion to identify your story and locate the help tip pages within that section, which you can apply to your situation today.

3. Pressed for time? Go to **THE CAREGIVER'S GUIDE** portion of the book to take in the self-care aspects to learn about the ways Health Coach Elaine suggests you go about building your own personalized self-care routine.

Foreword

What do you do when someone you love is in distress and you feel powerless to stop him or her? I watched Elaine change over the period of several years as she cared for her aging mother, affectionately known as "Grandma Lucy."

Grandma Lucy was a pistol from start to finish, that's for sure. I watched Elaine wait on her hand and foot and my heart hurt because I saw how much of a strain it was on her.

When I talked to Elaine, she had a sense of futility about the situation, as if there was no one or no thing that could relieve her burden. That's when I knew she was in big trouble.

As a Life Coach, I've learned that as hard as it is to accept sometimes, we truly do create our own reality with our thoughts and beliefs. If you feel there is no help and no hope, then that is what you will see in your world.

It was clear to me that Elaine and her mother Lucy had entered into some kind of unconscious contract, where Lucy demanded and Elaine provided. I also saw that it was killing Elaine to fulfill that contract but she would not let it go. I believe that we are divine beings having a human experience and wellbeing is our birthright. But what do you do when your wellbeing is directly impeded, by caring for a loved one? Most of the time, out of a sense of duty, the caregiver sets their wellbeing aside for the sake of another. Of course, this is not a conscious choice, which makes it even more insidious.

Not everyone is cut out to be a caregiver! When we have children, we are biologically driven through hormones and other physiological responses to care for our children and provide for them at all costs. When a parent ages, the caregiver often feels as though they should feel the same way about their parent and provide for them the way their parent cared for them in their childhood.

But hormones don't work backwards. To care for an aging adult means you need to dig down deep and give more than you feel capable of at times. But it's those unconscious contracts we create with each other that can do serious damage to the psyche. Guilt trips, anger and resentments that build up over the years can drip poison into day-to-day life and that is nothing short of destructive.

If caregiving is literally killing you as it was killing Elaine, that may be why you picked up this book. You have come to the right place! Elaine has a unique blend of love, commitment and good old-fashioned dogged perseverance that caused her to journey with her mother the way she did.

Learn from her journey.

I remember the day I knew she had turned a corner. The struggle between her and her mother had dissipated. They seemed at peace with each other. It was beautiful to watch them the last few months and it put me at ease to see Elaine more relaxed.

There is no living without dying. There is no dying without living. But it's up to us to create the quality of our journey. If you feel like you are simply not cut out to be a caregiver, you may just be right. Examine the unspoken contracts you have with your aging parent. Decide whether or not those contracts are healthy for you to keep. Those contracts usually sound something like, "A daughter should do..." "What kind of a son would I be if I didn't..." or "You're my child, it's your duty to wait on me the way I desire."

As Elaine learned, there are many different ways to be a caregiver. All of her wisdom is in the book. Take what works for you and trust your instincts. The most important thing to remember is that wellbeing is your birthright. There can be a mutually beneficial solution to any situation, but the key is to take care of yourself first and Elaine gives you numerous ideas in the book for how to do exactly that.

Be gentle with yourself and know that the most important thing you can offer is love and compassion, but that always starts with the self. Once you have filled your own well with love, self-care and compassion, you will have the energy to be present for all of the miracles that can unfold as you care for your aging parent and aid them in their passage to the other side.

What a gift that will be to them, to you, to your family and the world.

Be well.
Theresa S. Valenzuela
Author, Coach and Image Consultant
www.manwomancolor.com

Hurricane Lucy

"Courage does not always roar.
Sometimes courage is the quiet voice
at the end of the day saying,
I will try again tomorrow."

~Mary Ann Radmacher

CHAPTER 1

STORM CLOUDS

I 'll never forget what a social worker once told me, *"60% of caregivers end up becoming ill or dying while caring for a loved one."* The main cause of this statistic is stress.

Rarely are we ever prepared for walking into the role of being a caregiver to our own parent. It's a role that requires time, energy and attention, with seldom a break. Perhaps you were thrust into the role of being your parent's caregiver suddenly, without warning, due to their need for care after a debilitating fall or diagnosis of a chronic illness. Or maybe you were eased into it over time as it became more evident that their need for help had increased. Either way, you came to the realization that your aging parent could no longer handle daily tasks safely on his or her own. This pulled at your heartstrings with an overwhelming sense of responsibility to step in.

There are few transitions in life more difficult than when a parent needs to give up his or her home and independence. Likewise, disrupting your own home and your own adult life to meet your parent's increasing need for assistance can be tumultuous.

Uprooting a parent by bringing him or her into your home can be audaciously disconcerting. They may become confused by the changes they are experiencing and all the decisions being made for them. During this difficult time of vulnerability and adjustment, a very delicate role change shifts between you, as the adult-child and your parent. As you step in to help your parent may become impatient, irritable, nasty and demanding. They may reject everything you are trying to do for them, which may cause you to feel unappreciated. Their lack of respect or resisting your help can be disheartening.

Our parents were capable of doing their own thing day after day, year after year and decade after decade. It can be devastating for them to accept and overwhelming for them to understand why they are being kept from doing their own thing now. Balancing a parent's need for independence while keeping him or her safe is difficult to pull off.

An elderly parent can become resentful and fearful, which is understandable. They are told that it's time to fill out an Advance Directive and assign someone a Power of Attorney to act on their behalf. How would you feel becoming physically frail and cognitively limited? Most people in that position would feel as though they were losing control of their lives.

As caregivers we often spend a lot of time grasping at straws. We try to find ways to alleviate the tension in our home caused by the tremendous amount of stress we are under. Taking care of an aging parent is very demanding physical and emotional work. As a caregiver it's common to neglect taking proper care of our own self. We tend to run ourselves ragged all day long taking care of our aging parent's surmounting needs. We can easily become sleep deprived from dealing with nighttime difficulties of our own and ones our aging parent may be experiencing. Continuing this pattern day after day and night after night can have a profound, negative impact on our own health.

As much as you may realize that you need to do something about it, the mere thought of putting another thing on your plate to do, even if for yourself, seems like too much. If you feel this way, I can honestly say that you are not alone. Over the years, my mother and I have been through times that can only be characterized as the good, the bad and the ugly.

As much as I love my mother and for the most part feel as though I have been a devoted daughter, some days it felt like I just wasn't cut out to be the kind of caregiver she expected me to be. I never wanted her to feel as if she was a burden to me, but in all honesty there were times when I felt as though she was a thorn in my side. That's such a terrible thing to say about a loved one, but roses have thorns.

All the power struggles I could not win coupled with feeling like a prisoner in my own home caused me to become depressed. All the extra work involved with trying to maintain a clean and sanitary household when my mother's incontinence made my husband and I feel as though we are living in a toilet was exhausting. Overworked, feeling totally disrespected, frustrated and completely stressed out eventually took its toll on me. That's when the unthinkable happened. I found myself slamming doors in the middle of the night in a fit of rage screaming, "I CAN'T DO THIS ANYMORE!"

In the blink of an eye my whole world seemed to have collapsed, when in reality it was years in the making. Something evil had slowly been seeping into the very core of my being. I no longer recognized the person I had become. I felt so overcome with a haunting shame I could not seem to shake. The profound guilt I felt from blowing up in the face of my frail helpless mother was so disturbing to me. I wished I could just run far, far away. But where would I go and with whom could I leave my mother? I felt there was no way anyone else would or could ever put up with her and her behavior. People just don't live like this, so why was I?

In my heart I yearned for feeling truly at home in my own skin again. In order to do so I'd have to figure out how to go from overwhelming stress to bringing the joy back into my life and loving, compassionate relationships back into our home.

Voicing my concerns to my mother fell on deaf ears. It's not enough to just want to understand something or simply settle for acceptance and making peace with whatever is going on. I believe that actions speak louder than words. I forced myself to act as if I was strong in the face of my weaknesses in order to resolve the problems we were having. As hurtful as we were to each other at times, I knew we wouldn't be yelling the way we had been if we didn't care about each other and our situation. Otherwise it would have been too easy to just walk away.

Help Tip:

Stress comes from how you respond to situations. So you do have some control over stress by how you allow it to affect you. Life's challenges can be very unsettling. Every situation is unique, but life can be lived to the fullest when you make life happen on your terms. The airlines got it right by instructing us to *"Put your own oxygen mask on first."* When you take the time to care for yourself first, you become better able to care for others.

Some of the warning signs of stress are:

- Unusual sadness, moodiness, anger or rage
- Social withdrawal from activities and friends
- Fatigue, exhaustion and difficulty sleeping
- Change in eating habits and weight
- Recurrent headaches, stomach aches and colds
- Difficulty concentrating on other areas of your life
- Unexplained irritability
- Feelings of dread, hopelessness and depression

Not all stress is bad. Stress can help protect you in dangerous situations. However ongoing, chronic stress can put you at risk for heart disease, obesity, high blood pressure, and depression.

Some stress is hard to avoid, but stress is manageable when you take control of managing it every day. In **The Caregiver's Guide** portion of this book you will find a checklist of stress relieving techniques to incorporate into your daily self-care routine.

"*Every one of us alone has the power
to direct the course of our lives
by choosing what actions
we will or won't take.
While sometimes it's easier
to believe you don't have a choice,
the reality is that
you always have a choice to
behave and think differently.*"

~Francine Wardi

CHAPTER 2

THE EYE OF THE STORM

"You chose this." Those three little words seemed to cut through me like ice. How could my son say such a thing to me?

Usually when a client comes into my office feeling upset about something, I ask them to recall what had happened just prior to them getting upset. For me, I recall how lovely it felt to have the warm ocean breeze caressing my skin again. My husband and I had gone out to lunch with our son Benjamin at a trendy beachfront restaurant the day before he was to leave on a business trip.

We were seated outside on the restaurant patio overlooking the ocean. I was being rather quiet, as I was not at all interested in listening to my husband tell our son about all the latest annoying things my mother had been doing. Lost in my own thoughts as I watched the ocean waves, reminded me of how much I used to love being at the beach. I hadn't come in such a long time. Being near the ocean always made me feel so free. In fact, whenever I meditate and go to my happy place, I always picture myself on the beach. I'm wearing a sheer, long, white flowing summer dress. As I dance barefoot on the sand with my arms outstretched wide, I welcome the sun as it shines through my wavy, sandy blond hair.

That day however, all of a sudden tears started to fill my eyes as if coming from a black cloud passing overhead. I was hoping that my son wouldn't notice, even though I was sure it was obvious, since my nose always turns a little red when I cry. I tried to just brush it off as feeling sorry for myself.

That's when my son said, "You chose this," followed by, "If you don't like it, make a change."

Aghast with emotion I tried to make sense of what he was saying. I can see how he believes that we make a choice everyday to live the way we do. After all, he lives a good life that way.

My situation was different though. I felt like lashing back by saying, "There is no way that I would ever choose to continue to subject myself and my husband to living with a mother like mine if I had a choice, not after what she has been putting us through. I had no choice! My mother had no place else to go. What was I supposed to do, just throw her out in the street?" But I held my tongue.

At first glance it would appear as though I had no choice. I grew up in a close-knit Italian family where it is customary during old age for the parent to move in with a family member, usually their daughter. It honestly never occurred to me that it would be any other way. When the time came, my mother moved in with me and I accepted the passing of the baton as my turn without question.

In a way, I was being groomed for this role throughout my life. I watched my mother take care of my grandfather when he lost his leg, due to diabetes. Several years later when my grandmother became ill, I shared my bedroom with my grandmother while my mother lovingly took care of her too.

What could I possibly say to Benjamin to make him fully understand the situation? Deep down I knew what he was getting at and I understood he didn't like seeing me so unhappy. At the same time, I just couldn't accept the fact that I chose this for my life. Those three little words seemed to have seeped in through the crevices of my skin to haunt me.

Often other people can see for us what is hard for us to see for ourselves. My son saw how trapped and stressed out I was. I knew his words were not meant to be hurtful. He was simply expressing the fact that he was concerned about me. All the complaining my husband was doing just compounded the situation. I don't blame him either, since I complain about my mother too sometimes.

It took months to figure out why I had become so upset by those words. Then it hit me. I felt like the victim. I've seen it so many times in my health coaching practice. A sure sign of being stuck in victim mode is when you have the need to complain about something you feel as though you have no control over. I had become so focused on all the details that were upsetting me about how my mother was treating us that the whole picture wasn't coming into focus. I couldn't see the forest for the trees. I had to finally stop and ask myself, "Who's in control of my life?"

The thing that irked me the most was when my mother would say "it's my duty to do everything she asks me to do, no matter what it is, simply because I am her daughter." In what rulebook or stone tablet is that written as one of the commandments?

In many ways I had become the typical burnt-out caregiver. Hearing those three little words, "you chose this" was my breaking point. We all have our breaking points. Instead of dwelling on them we can use them to turn our life around, and that was exactly what I needed to do for myself.

My mother was the oldest of three sisters and two foster sisters. She was considered the matriarch of the family and never left home. She married and raised my brother Eric and I in my grandparent's house that her mother later willed to her. My mother's whole life revolved around her family.

There were many times when I'd come home from school to see my mother and my aunts gathered around our dining room table rolling out the dough to make homemade pasta together. It seemed like they were always complaining about the problems they were having with their husband's. Afterwards, I'm pretty sure they went home and pretended as if everything was fine in their homes.

My father was a quiet man. He rarely ate at the same table with the rest of the family. He was a meat and potatoes kind of guy and my mother usually served him a separate meal in the living room on a TV tray. He worked long hours as an auto mechanic in a gas station. He was loyal to the company he worked for, keeping the same job for as long as I can remember. After work he liked to go drinking at one of the local bars in town. My mother would often wake my brother and I, in the middle of the night to take us with her, searching for him from bar to bar to bring him home. On weekends he liked spending time in the backyard shed that he used as a darkroom. He spent hours in there developing the black and white photographs he took with his 35mm camera.

The Guilt Trip

Help Tip:

Parents are notorious for laying guilt trips on their children. No one in this world knows your emotional buttons like your parent does. When they move in with you, they lose the one thing that they've always had over you: their authority. That's not easy to give up. They are bound to push your buttons as they attempt to re-establish their dominance over you.

Likewise, siblings and other family members may also know what some of your strengths and weaknesses are. Feeling disrespected, unappreciated and taken advantage of can weigh you down. We can use guilt as a way to examine our behavior and our reaction to it. This perspective will help you gain more control over the situation.

Healthy ways to use guilt wisely:

- Guilt has the potential to help you grow and mature. Use guilt as a warning sign that serves a purpose. Ask yourself if what you are feeling is rational or irrational.
- When guilt gets your attention, learn from it. Use feeling guilty to make a change, make amends, or let go of someone or something.
- Accept the fact that nobody is perfect. Everyone makes mistakes. Playing the woulda, coulda, shoulda game is self-destructive. Use guilt to help you make decisions for future behavior. After that, let it go.
- Guilt, no matter how it is dished out can become a habit. Determine whether or not it's coming from a place of habitual discontent.

My brother had very little respect for our father. I never got to know the man well enough to form an opinion. From as far back as I can remember our mother drilled it into us that our father was a drunk. I got the message loud and clear to stay away from him. I would have liked to be called "little princess" by my father, but that was something that never happened. Growing up in a large Italian family it was also very chaotic in our house. My mother, father, brother and I never had our own family time together.

I was the only girl cousin for the first thirteen years of my childhood and more of a tomboy than a girlie-girl. Being shy and quiet, I was teased by other's who'd say, "Cat got your tongue?"

The thing that I believe negatively affected me the most growing up was my mother making the mistake to have me repeat second grade unnecessarily. We had changed schools because my brother wasn't doing well. I overheard the conversation my mother had with the principal about my brother needing to repeat fourth grade. My mother decided it would be best for Eric's emotional wellbeing, to continue to keep us two grades apart. Knowing this made me feel like her second-class child, which hurt my self-esteem. By being a year older than my classmates, I felt as though I didn't fit in. In fact, the whole boob and period thing was rather traumatic for me, because I was the only girl going through all that stuff a year before any of the other girls in my class did.

There were lots of good times though. I played baseball in the street with my cousins and we made skateboards out of old metal skates that we'd ride down the hilly street we grew up on. My mother often took my brother and I to the library so he could catch pollywogs in the pond, located in the back of the library and I could borrow storybook record albums. Bambi was my favorite one. Afterwards we'd go to the Italian market to buy salami and the bakery for rolls to make sandwiches for our picnic in the car. Afterwards, we'd go to Thrifty's for an ice cream cone. We had the best park near our house. When both the swimming pool and the craft booth were open, my brother and I would spend the whole day at that park. I also took tap and ballet lessons there.

My mother didn't have many friends. The couple of women she became friends with were hand-me-down friends her sisters had introduced her to. I remember how she resented not being invited to some of the parties her sister Ann and her husband threw. She felt it was because they didn't want her drunken husband to go and ruin their parties. My mother, being manipulative and controlling, would sometimes just show up uninvited anyway.

My mother was a very enterprising woman, always finding ways to use her house to make extra money. After my grandparents passed away my mother converted the back den and dining room into a licensed preschool. She also developed an afterschool program to accommodate the children that stayed in her care beyond their preschool years. I often marveled at how creative she was coming up with different projects for them to do. They weren't the typical paper, scissors and glue craft projects most schools offer. Instead, she taught the children attending her afterschool program how to make useful things out of wood, like stools they could sit on or birdfeeders to hang outside. I wouldn't be surprised if the lumberyard had a special bin of scrap wood with her name on it, put aside just for her to rummage through.

My mother was also a very generous woman. In an effort to help my husband and I save money for a down payment on our first house, my mother allowed us to move into her house with our four small children while she rented a smaller house nearby that was just large enough to accommodate her and my father as well as run her childcare business. She was such a wonderful grandma to our children. Some of our children's fondest childhood memories took place in that house. My mother always was a kid magnet. She'd say, "Having children around keeps you young." And she looked very young for her age too.

Everyone: family, friends and even the cashier at the grocery store called her "Grandma Lucy." I did too sometimes. It's just who she was to everyone: Grandma Lucy. So how the heck did she go from affectionately being known as Grandma Lucy to having earned the title "Hurricane Lucy?"

I believe my mother has always been a force to be reckoned with. I've often witnessed her behavior to be non-compliant, disrespectful and inconsiderate. Confrontational and abrasive, she once threw a cooked roast over the counter at the butcher, accusing him of not selling her the choice meat she paid top dollar for.

As strong-willed as she was though, she was a fearful, overly cautious person who didn't trust easily. She was overly protective of her family and seemed to be on guard and suspicious of being taken advantage of. She was a perfectionist and wanted things done exactly the way she felt they should be. She always did her own thing, her own way, on her own terms and timetable.

I want to believe that my mother did her best to live up to being a kind, loving and generous person. So, I'll give her the benefit of the doubt because there are always two sides to a coin.

Even though she was such a forceful person on the outside I sensed she was lonely and hurting on the inside. I honestly believe she ignored the destructive path of her own insecurity, which most likely was the driving force that fueled Hurricane Lucy.

Family Dynamics

Help Tip:

The way a family lives and interacts creates the dynamics of that family. Family dynamics are influenced by factors, such as birth order, gender, parenting practices and socio-economic status. Within the family, role are created to coexist harmoniously, each assigned to certain duties.

- **Adjuster - Lost Child**
  This child escapes by daydreaming and withdrawing. As adults they tend to become actors and writers who express emotions while hiding behind their characters.
- **Acting out - Scapegoat**
  The scapegoat gets attention the only way they know how: negatively. As an adult they can be cynical, distrustful and self-destructive.
- **Responsible - Family Hero**
  This is the good student, sports star, and prom queen striving to make adults proud. As an adult they may be rigid and judgmental of others and secretly judge themselves as well.
- **Mascot - Caretaker**
  This child takes responsibility for the emotional wellbeing of the family. As adults they often go into helping professions. They have difficulty receiving love. They only know how to give it.

Roles acquired during childhood can affect conscious choice later in life. Nothing is black and white. In co-dependent families problems develop when one family member takes on the role of meeting another family member's personal needs. Changing patterns from your past is not easy but by realizing who you truly are, not how you or your parent needed you to be, change is possible.

"As a single footstep will not make
a path on the earth,
so a single thought will not
make a pathway in the mind.
To make a deep and physical path,
we walk again and again.
To make a deep mental path,
we must think over and over
the kind of thoughts we
wish to dominate our lives."

~Henry David Thoreau

CHAPTER 3

HURRICANE FORCES

My mother was definitely a go-getter who thrived on being a problem solver. Although her expectations were high for others, when it came to taking care of herself her personal standards were low. In fact, I wouldn't be surprised if her sister Barbara had my mother in mind when she wrote the children's story, "Aggie Baggie Mc Gee, Tralee."

Oh, how my mother loved the children's stories Barbara had written in hopes to get them published one day. When my mother became involved in helping her, she poured her heart, soul and money into doing everything she could to help. My mother wanted so much to see her sister realize the dream of being a published author one day. Sadly, her sister passed away before publishing any of them.

When I was born my mother asked my Aunt Barbara if she could use the name "Elaine," which was the name my aunt had picked for the daughter she never had. I think I felt closer to this aunt than I did to my other aunts for that reason.

After my father passed away, twenty-eight years ago, my mother stayed with us on and off. She was barely sixty at the time, still driving and certainly didn't need a caregiver. She closed her childcare business to turn her house into a rooming house for adults. It didn't take her long to renovate that three-bedroom house into seven separate living quarters. She converted the den, dining room and living room into four more bedrooms with a hallway between them leading to bathrooms and a large kitchen for residents to use.

Although she kept one of the bedrooms as her own private residence she preferred living like a gypsy, sporadically visiting with one family member after another.

She kept that house for the next ten years. Once she decided to sell it she asked me to promise that there would always be a place for her in our home, because one of her biggest fears was being placed in a nursing home. When I agreed to that promise, I didn't realize how much of a life sentence I had committed myself to.

"Change can be beautiful when we are brave enough to evolve with it, and change can be brutal, when we fearfully resist."

~Bryant Mc Gill

CATEGORY 1: Tropical Wave

My husband retired early, at the age of fifty-four. Three of our four children were married and our youngest Devin was eighteen and would also soon be leaving the nest.

The housing market was going crazy that year. Selling our home while the prices were so high afforded us the opportunity to purchase a brand new home and live debt free for the first time in our lives by moving out of Southern California. The idea of living in an area where we would experience more of Mother Nature's changing seasons, appealed to us.

We took a couple of RV trips across the U.S., visiting every state except Alaska and Oklahoma and decided to move to the beautiful town of Coeur d'Alene, Idaho. Even though my husband had retired, retirement was the farthest thing from my mind. I had recently lost 135 pounds, went back to school to take a certification course through the Institute of Integrative Nutrition and wanted to open my own health coaching practice. The Pacific Northwest seemed like the perfect place to do so with clean, fresh crisp mountain air, up in "God's Country," as the locals call the panhandle area of Northern Idaho. My husband looked forward to playing golf with his brother who had moved to Coeur d'Alene with his wife and daughter nine years prior.

My mother did not want to move from Southern California. Instead of coming with us she decided to move in with her sister Barbara.

We purchased a four-bedroom house in a neighborhood that could have come right out of the children's story, "The Country Mouse and The City Mouse." In the new planned community in which we lived, to the right was the city and to the left was the country. On any given day we could either turn right to buy milk and eggs at a local grocery store in the city or turn left to milk a goat or cow and chase chickens around a barnyard to gather eggs at local farms in the country.

After we had moved, my mother came up for a visit. I noticed how much she had slowed down since the last time I saw her. After all, two little old ladies in their mid-eighties, both in the walker brigade, being left alone to fend for themselves was not an ideal situation. We all agreed that it was time for her to settle down by moving in with us permanently.

We had a bit of a dilemma on our hands. Purchasing a home without a downstairs bedroom made it challenging to accommodate my mother's disability needs. My mother was a heavy-set woman. She had extremely large arms, which weighed her down. Having such heavy arms made it difficult for her to hold her back up straight. She used to place her forearms on top of the walker she purchased for support, which caused her lean over even further.

Due to her carrying around so much weight, she also had weak knees. She walked very gingerly and was unable to comfortably lift her legs high enough to climb the stairs in our house without putting forth quite a bit of effort. In an attempt to make climbing a full flight of stairs a little easier for her we placed 12 inch 4"X6" wooden blocks on each step to create half steps for her. She did okay climbing up all those half steps, however it wasn't the safest method. Plus it was taking her forever to get up and down the stairs as we waited by her side monitoring her every step of the way. It didn't take us long to bite the bullet and order an electric chairlift for the stairs. It wasn't the prettiest sight, but it was so much more convenient.

We then addressed the obstacles we came across her having in the kitchen. My mother could not reach the controls on the back of the stove or reach the microwave above. She also couldn't reach the kitchen sink faucet to turn the water on and off. The solution we came up with was to convert one of the two extra upstairs bedrooms into a kitchenette for her. We equipped it with a small sized refrigerator, a microwave and a few small electric appliances. There was room enough for her to have a comfortable chair and a TV as well. She used her bathroom sink to obtain any water she needed for cooking. Even though I cooked and we all ate dinner downstairs together most of the time, she liked feeling independent in her own little apartment upstairs.

It took her awhile to adjust to the cold climate during the winter. She enjoyed looking out the window at the picturesque changing seasons and spent time reading. Little by little she was getting to know a few of the neighbors. She seemed content, but I sensed she missed the family she had left behind in Southern California, especially her oldest great granddaughter Sara, who had moved to Southern California from Maryland after dropping out of high school.

My mother encouraged Sara to go to a trade school by offering to help pay for half of her tuition. My mother didn't have a lot of money, but she knew how to make it stretch. She was always very generous with it when it came to helping family. The only stipulation was you had to come up with your share before she would match it and prove that any money she gave you would be used to better your life in some way. There was no way she was about to frivolously give away money to just buy you a pair of shoes. Those shoes had to be ones that you could prove would take you farther in life walking in them, than you could walk without them.

Moving to a new state meant that my mother would need to sign up for a local Medicare supplement health insurance plan. We choose a doctor for her that specialized in geriatrics and afforded her the opportunity to get some much needed physical therapy to strengthen her back and knees. This doctor was very impressed with how sharp she was for her age and encouraged her to strive to reach her goal to walk without a walker. It pleased me to see her getting the type of medical attention and care that I wish she had gotten years ago.

My mother stayed very focused on her goal, working diligently in the therapy pool and in the gym with the physical therapists. Her doctor also referred her to a massage therapist. Nine months later she had progressed to walking with two canes and was able to finally throw her walker away. She bought herself a power scooter to drive around the neighborhood and loved driving it downtown to go shopping.

 She happened to stop in a church one day that was having an after service soup and salad luncheon. They were about to serve dessert as she strolled in the meeting hall where they invited her to join them. Every Sunday she went down to join the friends she was making by attending those soup and salad luncheons. She was soon getting invited to get together with some of the girls to play Bunco and Mexican train. She joined the Red Hat Society and the friends she made there nicknamed her LuLu Bell.

On her eighty-eighth birthday I invited her new friends to a tea party at our house. In a relatively short two-year period, it seemed as though my mother was emerging from the cocoon she had been living in all her life to turning into a beautiful butterfly. Changing her environment was good for her. She no longer needed to be the one who fixed everyone and everything in order to feel needed. I think it quite possibly was the first time in her life she took the initiative to live her own life.

I was busy with my health coaching practice, my husband played golf with his brother, and we enjoyed getting together with our own friends. My mother making friends of her own was our saving grace. By her not being so needy, made the times we were able to spend together less burdensome and more enjoyable for all of us.

Sara was pregnant when she came up to visit the following spring. Shortly after baby Sophie was born, Sara and her boyfriend moved from Southern California to Las Vegas, Nevada.

When my mother flew down to visit Sara and see her first great-great grandchild, Sara invited her to move in with them. My mother phoned me to tell me that she wouldn't be coming back anytime soon. She explained that Sara needed help with the rent and also help with the baby. I had my reservations about her returning to a position of being needed like that, but I was happy for her at the same time too. I knew how much she loved being around children.

Each time we spoke on the phone my mother said everything was going well for her in Las Vegas. The apartment they shared was located around the corner from a large shopping center with stores she said she enjoyed shopping in. She was enjoying the baby and getting along well with Sara's boyfriend Carl.

When I went down for a visit I discovered that the things my mother was telling me were only half-truths. Although she seemed to be thriving emotionally very well in that environment, she was on the decline physically. On the phone she never once mentioned that she had reverted back to using a walker. That was disappointing for me to see, especially since she had worked so hard to walk without one using canes. It also became obvious to me that even with using a walker for support and balance, it had become increasingly more difficult for her to get around.

When I asked her if she talked to her doctor in Las Vegas about getting some physical therapy, she shrugged it off. She said she had a membership at a gym she could use, but admitted she hadn't taken advantage of going yet. Her excuse was that she didn't like having to wait for the bus to bring her and take her back home.

She insisted she was happy living there. I could tell how much she was enjoying little Sophie and I didn't have the heart to ask her to come back home. It was a lively house with Sara's cousin Nicole visiting often as well as their other friends popping in for barbecues and hanging out to watch movies together. My mother showed me the portable scooter that Carl kept in the trunk of his car. She said it came in handy when Carl and Sara took her with them out to dinner or downtown to the Las Vegas Strip to see a show or do a little gambling.

We celebrated my mother's ninetieth birthday, family reunion style in Maine at my daughter Emily's house. My daughter's husband James built their home on a twenty-seven-acre piece of property that James' grandmother had sold to them shortly after they were married. James had a large family in Maine. They were able to accommodate everyone that flew up for her birthday celebration.

For the party James' relatives brought over big outdoor electric pots to cook the sweetest, freshest Maine lobsters and clams he could get by going down to the boat docks. It was a beautiful day in August and my mother was delighted to see that so many relatives were able to come. Their presence made it a very special day.

The following day we all drove down to Portland and took a ferry to visit one of the nearby islands. Once we arrived we rented a wheelchair for my mother with each of us taking turns wheeling her around the island the whole day, which wasn't easy, considering all the hills we went up and down.

My mother looked a little tired that week, which was understandable, especially after traveling and needing to acclimate to the time difference between the west and the east. So we took it a little easier the rest of the week. During the day we walked out back into the forest while James drove her in his truck so we could all pick and eat the wild blueberries straight from the bush. In the evening we sat around their fire pit to roast marshmallows for the S'mores we made. We played games, made some of our old family favorite recipes and even tried something new: grilled pizza cooked on the barbeque. It was fun having the whole family together again like that.

Little Sophie stuck to her Grandma Lucy like glue the entire week. They were so cute together and it was obvious how close they had become. Before they left to return to Las Vegas Sara told me that she had gotten a job working at a beauty salon. She also mentioned that Sophie was going to be starting preschool in September and Grandma Lucy was looking forward to volunteering at the preschool.

Two months later I got the call.

Overbearing Parents

Help Tip:

If your overbearing parent is anything like mine was, he or she may be using controlling behavior as a cover-up for his or her own insecurity. I've learned a thing or two about ways to cope with an overbearing parent that I'll share with you here.

Dealing with overbearing parents:

- Did you spend your childhood seeking approval from your parents? If so it's time to let go of your need to please. If you haven't won your parents over by now you're just holding onto a fantasy that isn't realistic. Just know; that all parents love their children even when they don't show it.
- Overbearing parents usually demand all the attention. They don't like too many other people in the picture. If they attempt to persuade you from getting close to others, the best thing to do is assure them that you value their opinion but prefer to make your own judgment calls. Doing so will quiet them, but be aware they may not let the issue rest easily.
- An overly protective parent may be afraid you will fail without their intervention. They may feel the need to involve themselves in every aspect of your life. Stand up for yourself as an adult by making your own decisions. It's your life, not theirs.
- It's futile thinking that you can change your parent or wish their manipulative behavior away. The best thing to do is change your reaction to it. Keep this quote in mind: *"The cause of every change comes from within, never from without."* ~ *Andrew Lombardi*

"The happiest people don't always have the best of everything, they just make the most of it."

~Anonymous

CATEGORY 2: Tropical Disturbance

"I don't know what's wrong with Grandma Lucy," my frantic niece Sara cried into the phone.

"We called the paramedics when she started slurring her words, but she wouldn't go to the hospital in the ambulance. I drove her here when they indicated that she should be seen. She's screaming at the doctors and nurses, totally freaking out," she cried.

I could hear my mother screaming hysterically in the background. She was yelling at the nurse to take the side rails down.

"Let me talk to one of the nurses," I said.

I explained to the nurse that my mother was very claustrophobic and needs the side rails down immediately. I was afraid she'd have a heart attack from becoming so upset. The nurse emphatically exclaimed it was against hospital policy.

In the background I heard my mother calling out my name.

"Elaine. Elaine. I won't fall out. Please tell them to put the railing down. I can't stand it in here any longer. I want to go home. Please come here. Please help get me out of here!" she called out.

"Were you able to run the tests she needed to have?" I asked.

"Yes. Your mother's sodium levels are very low. We have her on IV fluids and Dr. Kim wants to keep her overnight for observation. She is insisting that she has the right to sign herself out, which she can certainly do, however it would be against doctors orders," she explained.

"Can you please put her on the phone?" I asked.

My mother would not listen to reason. She was hysterical. It was obvious that everyone was going to have a long night if she stayed there. After talking to Sara again, we decided that it would be best to just let her sign herself out. I assured Sara that I would come to help take care of my mother for a couple of weeks, but after that, it would be best if she came back home with me.

I drove my RV down to give myself a comfortable place to live in, while I was there. I also wanted to be prepared to pack up her belonging in case we were successful in convincing her to come back with me.

When I arrived, my mother was home alone. She looked a little pale, which I suppose was to be expected after the ordeal she had gone through at the hospital. She said she hadn't been eating too well lately and asked me to make her some toast and coffee. I scrounged around in the kitchen looking for something more substantial for her to eat. The only nourishing thing I saw to make quickly was oatmeal. I sliced up a banana to put on top and also made her the piece of toast she wanted along with a cup of coffee. Since she was low in sodium I explained to her that it would be a good idea to sip some warm water with a pinch of pink Himalayan salt in it throughout the day. The minerals in the salt would help to balance her electrolytes.

Looking around, the house gave me the impression that Sara must have become very busy. There were dried up French fries on the kitchen table and piles of unfolded laundry thrown on the sofa. I know things can pile up sometimes, especially after starting a new job. That didn't bother me, but seeing a commode beside my mother's bed, did. I waited until she finished eating before asking her about it.

My mother was embarrassed to tell me about the accident she had a couple of weeks ago while on her way to the toilet. Sara had gotten mad about having to clean it up and Carl wasn't happy about it either. Using a commode in her room was easier for her.

I waited for Sara to come home from work before I left to go to the grocery store so I could make her the type of foods that I knew would help her regain her strength. I ended up living in my RV for the next eight months.

We had a pretty good routine going. I was probably spoiling her, but I enjoyed doing so. I made a crockpot full of homemade bone broth that I kept a in crockpot, served her healthy meals, high fiber black bean brownies and Greek yogurt cheesecakes as special treats. Two days a week I drove her to the senior center across town to use their therapeutic pool. Most afternoons my mother and I sat outside with our feet resting on the grass Earthing. Further information and how-to instructions about this technique and other beneficial one's, as well as my favorite healthy recipes, are located in **THE CAREGIVER'S GUIDE** portion of this book.

Sophie's preschool was seven short blocks from where they lived. Every Thursday my mother enjoyed riding her scooter there to help out. I went with her a few times. It warmed my heart to see the children run up to her the minute she arrived. They all naturally called her "Grandma Lucy." She watched the children play in the schoolyard and read to them during story time, according to the teacher's plan for the day.

My husband flew down a few times while I was there, but he never stayed too long. I on the other hand actually loved the Las Vegas area. After living in the cold Pacific Northwest, I felt sun deprived.

My mother had lost some weight but we were unsuccessful in getting the referrals she needed for the physical therapy I would have liked her to have. At least she wasn't walking as hunched over, while using her walker, after I adjusted it for her so she'd hold it with her hands instead of leaning so heavily on it with her forearms.

On occasion she'd get thrown off course when Carl and Sara brought junk food into the house. For the most part, she knew how to eat healthy and was capable of shopping and cooking for herself, in a little kitchen I helped her set up in her bedroom.

I happened to introduce myself to the Boy Scout leader next door and was invited to teach a Nutrition Detectives™ workshop at one of the troop meetings. One workshop led to another and before I knew it I was teaching workshops to other Scout troops, as well as in elementary schools and scheduling grocery store tours for parents.

I stayed through the end of May. Even if my mother would have agreed to come back with me I couldn't take her home just yet. I needed to leave to attend a business conference in New York City. I had also arranged a trip to Massachusetts to volunteer at the Kushi Institute located in the Berkshire Mountains.

The Kushi Institute is famous for their work treating cancer patients. It was a wonderful opportunity to learn more about the work they do and the role they believe the macrobiotic diets plays when treating cancer patients. I signed up to volunteer for a month in the facilities kitchen in exchange for taking some of the classes they taught at the Institute.

Four months after I returned home from my trip I got another call from Sara.

"Grandma Lucy hasn't been feeling well. She stays in bed complaining of back pain and her side bothering her. I can't take off work to take her to the doctor or stay home to take care of her. When can you come down again?" she asked.

I flew down the following day and made an appointment for her to see her doctor. After the examination and blood tests her doctor told us that her gallbladder was infected and suspected that a gallstone may have gotten lodged in a bile duct. At her age, she wasn't a candidate for surgery. The best course of action was to put her on antibiotics to try and get the infection under control. I needed to get back home. Sara told my mother that she doesn't feel comfortable leaving her home alone while she's at work and that it would be best if she went home to live with me.

My mother was not happy about being back in Idaho. The weather was starting to turn cold and she wasn't interested in contacting any of the friends she had made to let them know she was back. She preferred to stay upstairs reading by herself. I felt bad about her having to leave the life she had been enjoying in Las Vegas. I knew she missed Sophie and I'm sure she would have liked to continue to help out at the preschool. But my home was in Coeur d'Alene. My mother was ninety-one years old and none of us felt that it was a good idea for her to being staying home alone for so many hours a day while Sara was at work.

Despite having completed the round of antibiotics she was given, the discomfort she was experiencing persisted. I took her to the emergency room and she was admitted to the hospital a short time later. I stayed with her while she waited for a specialist that was called in to figure out what course of treatment to take.

The following afternoon her pain had subsided but she still hadn't seen the specialist or been given anything to eat or drink, not even ice chips. I was concerned that she would become dehydrated without fluids. The nurse on duty told me they could not do anything without the doctor first putting in an order. I became angry and accused the hospital of being neglectful, threatening to leave if she wasn't attended to within the hour. My mother was getting very impatient too. She wanted to leave. An hour and a half later I grabbed a wheelchair from the corridor and we escaped.

That evening the specialist finally called to say he had been delayed and for me to take her back to the hospital. After relaying the message to my mother, she told me she would only agree to see him in his office. I made the appointment with him for the following morning. During the appointment he gave her a shot along with prescribing a much stronger dose of antibiotics than she had taken before. Ten days later, her blood test results indicated that the infection had finally cleared up.

The winter red berries on the holly bush outside my kitchen window looked so beautiful with a dusting of snow. Christmas was right around the corner. The thought of just the three of us spending it without being surrounded by family, weighed heavily on my mind. I wanted to do something to cheer my mother up. We finally made last minute plans to spend Christmas in Maine. The liveliness of four of our grandchildren, Ryan, Susie, Taylor and Katie running around the house excited about opening presents was sure to put us all in the Christmas spirit.

We arrived at our daughter's house the week before Christmas. The following day my mother said she felt tired, which I thought might just be jetlag. That night she couldn't seem to settle down and complained that she had a pain on her side again and her back was hurting. As she talked I noticed her starting to slur her words quite a bit. Concerned that she may be having a stroke our son-in-law James, who is a paramedic, took her vital signs.

"She could just have a Urinary Tract Infection," he said and proceeded to arrange for an ambulance to take her to the hospital. As the night progressed it seemed like she was getting more and more delirious. The doctor ordered tests and what they discovered was not good. She was septic. An infection had spread throughout her entire blood system. After conferring with a couple other doctors they all came back in to tell me that my mother was in very serious shape. She was admitted to the intensive care unit and advised me I called the family.

Over the course of the next five days she was given large doses of medications to treat the infection. Luckily she responded well to these drug treatments. A tube was placed through her abdomen into her gallbladder to remove bile sludge.

I stayed with my mother, sleeping on a chair that folded out into a bed. My mother was in the hospital for five days, receiving excellent care.

Being in bed day after day like she was can cause a patient to lose quite a bit of muscle tone. I assisted her in moving her arms and legs while she lay in bed, but what she needed was to start doing some weight bearing exercises. I talked to one of the doctors about it and he agreed to order a physical and occupational therapist to come in to evaluate her. They were able to get her up walking a few steps with the assistance of a walker and holding a gait belt around her waist. They let me know that once she was released from the hospital she would receive home health care.

She was released on Christmas Eve, and we all enjoyed a festive Holiday together and decided to extend our stay in Maine for two more months. Our daughter found and purchased an electric lift chair for her grandma to make it easier for her to get up and down from a seated position. Through the services provided by the home health care agency, my mother received a nurse, a physical therapist, an occupational therapist, a bath aid and a social worker. Occasionally, a technician from the lab came to draw her blood.

She was getting stronger and did pretty well walking from the living room all the way down the hall and into the bedroom using her walker and having someone walking beside to hold the gait belt and encourage her to keep going. She could not be trusted to walk unattended anymore.

Sometimes she relied on getting around by riding her portable scooter in the house. She was a little reckless with it and toppled over twice while we were there by going around a corner to fast or running into one of the kid's snow boots or a toy that had been left on the floor.

James modified the wooden steps that led from their garage into the house to make it easier to get up and down them when she needed to be driven to a doctor's appointment. I emptied her drain tube two and three times a day for the following few weeks and I had to contend with emptying the bedside commode we finally went but to buy to make it easier for her to use during the night.

My mother enjoyed spending time with her great grandchildren. During the day they kept her entertained by performing magic tricks and playing checkers. Taylor was always running in the front door after school, ready with a new joke to tell her.

Nights were a completely different story. My mother was having a terrible time sleeping at night, and she wasn't being quiet about it, which became extremely annoying to everyone in the house. When I asked the doctor about it he explained that this can occur as a result of being awakened so many times during their stay in the hospital and that she may just need to adjust to a better schedule or because of her age, she may be experiencing Sundowners Syndrome. Giving her Melatonin, an over the counter sleep aid, helped when she would take it, but getting her to cooperate wasn't easy. I felt bad putting our daughter's family through all of this. We decided it was time for us to go home. But first, we needed to figure out how we could make it convenient for my mother to manage living in a two-story house since her disabilities had increased. Getting her a scooter for upstairs and downstairs was a thought, but the fact that she needed to constantly be reminded to turn it off before transferring from it onto a chair worried me. We weren't going to be able to trust her with a power scooter upstairs.

Our daughter suggested we look for a single story house to buy in Maine. At first, I really loved the idea of moving to Maine to be close to them. It would be great for our grandchildren to be able to come over anytime they wanted and the thought of having them over to bake cookies in my kitchen excited me. Plus, Emily was such a help to me with my mother. Despite the cold, I knew my mother would also love having the kids around all the time.

My husband and I went together to look at a few houses, but he always found something wrong with the ones we saw. But, the house my daughter and I came across really appealed to me. The house had recently been remodeled. Additionally there was a large separate storefront building located on the property, which could have easily been fixed up to become a yoga studio, as well as utilized to have workshops and maybe even teach cooking classes there. Unfortunately, my husband just couldn't quite wrap his head around moving from one cold climate to another with my mother. He felt that a better option for us would be to move back to Southern California. By doing so we'd still be living near two of our grandsons, Ronny and Ray. He also felt that the weather would be more conducive to the year round active lifestyle that we both were longing for once again, as we loved going on bike rides and I loved the sunshine.

Healthy living is a Choice

Help Tip:

Health is not simply the absence of sickness. According to the World Health Organization (WHO), Health is a state of complete physical, mental, and social wellbeing.

Health benefits and strategies I used with my mother are:

1. Healthy meals and snacks.
   a. Mineral rich homemade Bone Broth to help her fight infection, alleviate arthritic joint pain and reduce inflammation.
   b. Black Bean Brownies, which are loaded with protein and fiber.
   c. Greek Style Yogurt to provide her with healthy gut bacteria that is often lost from the use of medications, poor diet, diseases and toxins in the environment.
   d. Dark leafy greens and other colorful fruits and vegetables for their high vitamin content.

2. Warm therapeutic pool.
Getting into a pool provides seniors with limited physical abilities the opportunity to exercise their body without placing undue stress on their joints.

3. Earthing.
The sun and the earth have such healing powers. Earthing is a technique whereby you place your bare feet directly in contact with the earth. Doing so grounds you to the energy of the earth. Energy obtained from the earth has the potential to decrease inflammation, reduce pain, promote healthy sleep and thin the blood, which helps reduce heart disease.

"Sometimes the strongest among us are the ones that smile through silent pain, cry behind closed doors, and fight battles nobody knows about."

~Anonymous

CAREGORY 3: Tropical Depression

As soon as we got back home to Idaho we moved my mother's bed downstairs into the dining room and put our house up for sale. Have you ever tried to stage your home for sale with a bed and a bunch of handicapped paraphernalia in your dining room? Luckily we sold our house fairly quickly.

We headed down to Southern California where we leased a house in Laguna Woods Village, a gated, resort style 55+ community. At first my husband and I were like kids in a candy store. There are so many clubs and activities from which to choose. But, we couldn't very well leave my mother home alone while we were off partying all the time, so we picked just a few activities to keep ourselves active.

Within the first two months I landed a gig teaching a series of cooking classes. Doing so, led me to be interviewed by the host of a local TV program. By mentioning being the caregiver for my mother during the interview I started to get calls from other caregivers in the area. This opened my eyes to just how much we all had in common, which prompted me to start writing this book.

Helping my mother adjust to her new surroundings proved to be more difficult than I thought it would. One thing I neglected to notice before we moved in to this active community was that many of the sidewalks within the village are not equipped with handicapped ramps. This made navigating throughout the village difficult for my mother in her scooter. She managed by locating driveways leading out to the street she would ride along instead.

She ran into another problem. She was not able to reach the button to activate the crosswalk signal to make it safe for her to cross the street. Not pressing it did not allow her enough time to get across before the light turned red. I spent quite a bit of time instructing her to cross on the left side of the street so cars on the opposite side would see her if she didn't quite make it all the way across by the time the light changed. As I said before, my mother did her own thing her own way most of the time. This was no exception. Once after my husband and I had gone out shortly after she had we found her inching her way across the street. She was stopping traffic at every lane before proceeding to the next lane to get herself across the street.

It seemed like we were running into problem after problem with her. She didn't seem to be fitting in as we had hoped she would. I tried to interest her in some activities that I thought she'd enjoy. She would go a few times then she'd come up with excuses not to go. The only class she kept going to was the mind-fitness class. Well, at least doing one activity a week was better than nothing.

She complained of having difficulty making friends and seemed out of sorts. In an attempt to help her get the ball rolling to make some friends I accompanied her to some of the social events. It didn't take long for me to see what the problems were. It became apparent that a lot of the difficulty she was experiencing stemmed from her hearing difficulty. She had hearing aids, but resisted wearing them on a consistent basis.

Being confined to electric wheels affected her self-esteem and having such a negative attitude kept her socially isolated. I sensed something more was bothering her. She seemed very depressed.

My mother being the Captain of the boat on the River Denial would never admit to being depressed.

We were bucking heads more often than ever before. I don't ever remember seeing nor hearing my mother and grandmother yelling at each other the way we were going at it sometimes. Then again, I don't remember my grandmother ever being as much of a handful as my mother had become. That's no excuse for my behavior. I felt guilty about my outbursts and often wondered what was wrong with me for behaving in the way in which I had been.

Did we make the right decision bringing her back to Southern California? I knew that as wonderful as it once was the tide had changed. Her sister Barbara had passed away the year before and it was difficult for her to get together with other relatives unless I drove her.

Her grandchildren were good about calling her to keep in touch, which always lifted her spirits and she looked forward to the times our grandchildren Ronny and Ray visited. My mother and Ronny built a birdhouse together and she enjoyed watching him try his hand out drawing cartoons. I went to the Slip casting workshop to make clay molds, which I brought home for them to paint together.

I kept her as involved as I could, however looking into her eyes I sensed a deep sadness and loneliness. I felt as though my mother was not thriving well enough in the environment I tried so hard to provide for her. Seeing my mother decline in health and in spirit made me question whether or not it would be in her best interest for me to break the promise I had made to her years before. I wasn't sure anymore if I was doing the right thing, by making our home her home, instead of helping her find and adjust to living in an assisted living facility where she might to possibly receive more of what she needed.

But, whom was I kidding? I knew she'd never go, especially not after witnessing the way her sister Barbara was shuffled from one nursing home to another.

I believe nursing homes are as good as their staff. It's so difficult dealing with the demands and idiosyncrasies of elderly patients. A dedicated caregiver is necessary to lift, bathe and change diapers on a regular basis. Providing a safe environment is also a major concern. Pressure is placed on these facilities to comply with government rules and regulations. They are in business to make money and being required to accept a certain number of low income Medicare patients often times means having to cut costs to accommodate everyone that enters their door.

This was how my Aunt Barbara qualified to be in the ones she was placed in. She was shuffled around quite a bit. The first facility she was in was the nicest. I took my Aunt Ann and my mother to see her shortly after she moved there. During our visit we ate a lovely meal together in a dining room that resembled a fancy restaurant with cloth napkins. Our meal was served on china plates and waiters catered to our every request. Afterwards we were invited to join in the festivities in the recreation room, singing along as the piano player led the residents in song.

Her days were numbered in that facility, as they were in each of the subsequent facilities she was shuffled in and out of. Her health declining each time she was moved. She was soon diagnosed with having congestive heart failure and wasn't expected to live much longer. Congestive heart failure is the same disease that took my grandmother's life.

My mother could not bring herself to visit one last time. She told me she wanted to remember Barbara as she was in better days. I felt the need to say goodbye and show respect for the aunt that named me. I brought the folder my mother had given me containing the children's stories my aunt had written. While sitting beside her, reading all of them to her, there were moments I sensed she heard me and knew why I had come. I was there to tell her how much my mother and I loved her stories. I also wanted to convey to her my belief that one day, someone in her family would find the time to get them published in her memory. I felt it important to give her that one last joyful hope.

My mother-in-law's experience being in an assistant living facility was quite different. She was able to use the equity from the sale of her house to pay for her care. As a result, she wasn't moved from nursing home to nursing home. Like most, at first she was resisted going. After the initial adjustment period she seemed to like her new living arrangements. Everyone is different. Every place is different. Every situation is different.

It's difficult to make decisions for someone else's life. Yet that was what I found myself doing for my mother. The more demanding she became about doing things a certain way, the more difficult it became for me to go along with her when I didn't agree.

I was tired and she knew it. But we both knew there was no one else within the family that could accommodate her physical needs the way my husband and I had managed to do.

Several months after we moved, I don't know what may have happened, but something caused my mother to believe that we were being monitored, by living in an enclosed old people's community. She insisted that she knew that once you got in, you couldn't get out. She became extremely suspicious, accusing me of signing a paper that I didn't thoroughly read. None of what she was imaging was true, yet these thoughts fueled her paranoia to the point where they became all consuming.

Her doctor didn't think much of it and said that elderly people have a hard time with change and she just needed time to adjust. I also mentioned to him that she had been dropping things quite a bit. He said he noticed her hands were swollen which my mother insisted was normal for her because she had fat fingers like her mother's were. She also emphatically said she has carpal tunnel syndrome. What he didn't say and what I didn't realize was that it could have been a sign of her declining in health.

I kept pushing for more physical therapy. Her doctor warned me it was futile. Nonetheless, I insisted and he finally authorized eighteen more sessions at a nearby physical therapy clinic that offered transportation.

While on the bus, on the way home one day, the bus driver happened to make too sharp of a turn, which caused her to tip over in her scooter. After that happened the bus driver told me that he would not transport her again until she was in something more substantial. So, I found a used power chair for her. As it turned out the physical therapists said that she was sitting up better in the power chair than in the scooter and preferred she use it instead from then on.

My mother worked with more than one therapist and completed fifteen sessions before complaining that what they were having her do left her feeling too sore to continue.

"All these last-ditch efforts, besides not helping her, is taking its toll on you," my husband would say.

He was right. It had become too hard for me. I couldn't figure out why no one was being successful in helping her, especially since she was walking six years prior when we were living in Idaho.

Her doctor as well as all the physical therapists she'd seen within the past year told me that she would eventually become bedridden. What they couldn't tell me was how to prevent it from happening.

"There's just nothing more we can do for her," they all said. One even had the nerve to say, "We are not maintenance people."

She was doing the best she could and I knew it. Her knees were in such bad shape. Another last-ditch effort was taking her to an orthopedic specialist to see if there was anything he could do for her. From her x-ray Dr. Friedman pointed out that on a scale from 1 to 10, with 10 being the worst, she was a 12. The only treatment he could offer her was to remove the buildup of fluid in her knees and give her cortisone shots. It seemed to help ease the pain she was experiencing while getting up and down to transfer herself from her bed or a chair onto her power chair, but it didn't help her to walk. She still needed my assistance.

I could have used some help getting her out of bed, washed, dressed and transferred into her power chair for the day. It would have been such a relief for me to have this kind of help, but unfortunately, I couldn't find an affordable agency to relieve me for the short amount of time I needed help.

It got to the point where I got up earlier and earlier in order to take a shower before Her Royal Highness needed me to wait on her. I hadn't realized just how grumpy I had become until my husband finally said, "I miss your smile."

I missed it too. I was gaining weight and looked pretty dumpy from wearing the same couple of outfits that still fit. Embarrassed by my appearance, slowly but surely I started to give up the activities I used to like doing, felt like I should put my business on hold for a while and I just withdrew from everything and everyone. I became socially isolated.

I resented being forced to give up my own life for my mother's. What made me feel even worse was watching other people enjoying the life they were freely living. When was it going to be my turn to live my own life?

I felt lost in my mother's shadow. Clearly I was in too deep, and needed to figure out where to draw the line of responsibility and get myself back in shape.

My mother's dependence on me had made it nearly impossible for my husband and I to go out together. The few times we attempted going out she'd call me on the phone every 15 minutes to tell me how lonely she was staying in the house all by herself and for us to get back as soon as possible. Having her constantly interrupting our attempt at a date night didn't make it pleasurable for us at all.

Other than my mother's clinginess, what irritated me most was how uncooperative and noncompliant she was. She didn't seem to understand when you are dependent on another person for your care being respectful of that person's time is the considerate thing to do. My mother had the nerve to say that all I was doing was treating her like a puppet. WOW. That's a pretty big slap in the face if you ask me.

People have to want what you offer or you end up driving each other crazy. Even if significant changes are made they don't stick unless the person you are trying to help sticks with it.

I put a lot of time and effort into helping my mother. I am not sorry I did, I'm just disappointed that she didn't appreciate it.

I finally came to the realization that I could not help her with all that she needed. Sometimes someone not as close to the situation can make better headway when dealing with a difficult person. It was time for me to back off and just be her daughter. Perhaps that's all she really wanted all along.

Caregiver Depression

Help Tip:

Caregiver depression isn't something you can simply "snap out" of. Left untreated it can lead to physical and mental health problems as well as affect the quality of care you provide for your loved one.

Things you can do to avoid caregiver depression are:
- Eat well-balanced meals.
- Find time to exercise and get enough sleep.
- Realize you are human. Let go of unrealistic expectations.
- Ask for help and accept help when offered.
- Lighten your mood with humor.
- Be grateful for what matters most to you.

Signs of caregiver depression:
- Sad, anxious, and decreased energy.
- Feelings of guilt, worthlessness or helplessness.
- Loss of interest in pleasurable hobbies or activities.
- Difficulty concentrating and making decisions.
- Insomnia, waking up during the night or excessive sleeping.
- Overeating or appetite loss.
- Persistent aches and pains, headaches or digestive problems.
- Thoughts of suicide or suicide attempts.

If you are experiencing any of the above signs of depression, start by talking to someone about how you are feeling. Often simply talking things over with another person will help alleviate depression. If you think you may be suffering from a more serious clinical depression, seek medical attention from a professional.

"When something bad happens,
you have three choices.
You can either let it define you,
let it destroy you,
or you can let it strengthen you."

~Anonymous

CATEGORY 4: Tropical Storm

Everything in our house seemed as though it was in such disarray. The extra work involved with caring for my mother's basic needs was not the problem. The problem was she was impatient and uncooperative. It was difficult dealing with the craziness associated with feeling as though she did not trust me.

My mother was getting older and I knew it, but I wasn't accepting it. I was holding on to what once was. That was not fair to her, but I felt so strongly neither was just giving up on her. The question became, who should hold the reins?

I was not clear as to what should and shouldn't be expected from a ninety-two year old. My mother has always been very sharp for her age, stubborn as hell, but very wise and aware. In fact, the thought crossed my mind that maybe she had developed an extra sense to compensate for her disabilities. She sure was capable of getting herself out of many jams.

She was also very innovative when it came to trying to make things easier for herself. She liked using a long metal tong she called her picker-upper, to reach for things. In order to get a better grip on whatever she needed to grasp, she wrapped rubber bands around the ends of the tong. She placed hooks around her room to make it easier for her to hang up her clothes, instead of putting them on a hanger, even though we had moved the closet pole down lower for her to reach.

So many things needed to be modified for her. Our son Devin made a step stool for her, so her feet wouldn't hang when sitting in a chair high enough for her to get in and out off easily without putting to much strain on her knees. Whenever we went somewhere new I'd call ahead to make sure it was handicapped accessible. And *oh my gosh* there are so many restrooms that have such low toilets. There I'd be standing in front of her, lending her my body to hold onto for support, so she could stand straddling the toilet seat. You know, you have to laugh at some of these things, because if you don't you'd go crazy. Seriously though, it is so difficult for a handicapped person to maneuver around some of the obstacles they are faced with.

Despite having quite a bit of physical therapy she never regained the mobility she had prior to moving to Las Vegas. I thought her increasing immobility was due to muscle weakness until I noticed how her communication response time was slowing down as well. My mother was also becoming much more fearful. Could she have fallen prey to having some type of dementia? I wasn't sure.

"She's too sharp to have dementia," her doctor told me. Followed by, "Even if she does there is no cure and medications have very little to offer dementia patients."

I found myself searching for answers and came across an article written by Dr. Mark Hyman, M.D. He states, "The healing process is rather rudimentary. Recent research is indicating that when caught early enough, by attending to "all" the factors that affect brain function: diet, exercise, stress, nutritional deficiencies, toxins, hormonal imbalances and inflammation, the body will heal itself. You will get rid of the imbalances in the body as you re-plenishing it with all the building blocks for good health."

As a health coach I am well aware that most imbalances are caused by poor diet, toxins, inflammation and poor digestion. Re-plenishing the body with high quality nutrition along with healthy lifestyle habits was what I had been trying to provide for my mother, but why wasn't she responding?

As much as I tried to help her, "all" the factors: diet, exercise, stress, nutritional deficiencies, toxins, hormonal imbalances and inflammation were not "all" being addressed to work synergistical-ly together. My mother needed a team of professionals, all work-ing to help her help herself. She had that team of professionals as well as the attitude and gumption necessary to make that happen six years ago. That's what I knew, that's what I saw and that's why I kept forging forward. But looking back now, six years is a long time ago for a ninety-two year old and a lot had happened since then.

It's difficult to work with a person who is uncooperative. Throw in a little mistrust, season with paranoia, add a dash of for-getfulness, and you have the beginnings of getting nowhere near any sense of cooperation. It's a hard trek up a very slippery slope.

My mother kept upping the ante with an increasing need for more and more help. Honestly, it made my head spin and my heart ache for her.

She wasn't sleeping well. She was becoming extremely terrified. She feared that someone was going to come in the house and take her away against her will. She saw shadows running up and down the hall and heard people talking that weren't there. My husband and I could hear her late at night pleading with the shadows she sensed were in her room to leave her alone. She even offered them money to go away.

We called the help line and they told us to not engage in it but simply try to distract her away from her thoughts. Easier said than done. My mother wanted us to believe her, but I didn't know how. My husband was better at pacifying her in that way than I was.

Over the next few months the intensity increased. She had gone so far as to call 911 in the middle of the night to let them know that she was in danger. I heard her tell them that she wants to file a report stating that she's not crazy. She also called relatives, pleading with them to find a way to rescue her before it was too late. Can you imagine being 3,000 miles away, getting awakened in the middle of the night by a loved one saying that someone is planning to kill you?

When a person gets so wound up like that they can't listen to reason. I didn't feel changing the subject to distract my mother worked well enough. Maybe I just wasn't good at it. I preferred to solve the problem using preventative tactics.

I looked back to see if I could figure out what could possibly have happened just prior to her progressing into fits of paranoia. I concluded she wasn't sleeping well. Realizing this, gave me something to work with.

It would be important for my mother to wind down in the evening. It wasn't always easy but it was definitely worth the time and effort it took to get into a better nighttime routine. I started by dimming the lights, shutting the TV off and turning the radio on a soft music station. Once she was in bed most nights I gave her a warm soothing bed bath. She loved getting powdered up with the cooling, soothing affects of cornstarch after her bath. I'd put a drop or two of calming lavender essential oils on her pillow and caressed the top of her head. Simply sitting beside her bed holding her hand as she fell asleep worked wonders.

Did this work all the time? No. On two separate occasions she wouldn't allow me come near her, let alone touch her, in order to help her out of the living room chair and into bed. She insisted on sitting up keeping watch all night. The only thing I could do at that point was dim the lights and turn the TV off in hopes she would become so bored and fall asleep. It took her an entire week to recuperate from the affects of what staying up all night did to her system.

Our son Jason happened to meet Ted, the CEO of the Alzheimer's Association, at a business event he attended. He suggested I call to make an appointment to get some advice.

Both Ted and a social worker named Karen, met with me to discuss what was going on and to talk about the symptoms my mother was experiencing. The meeting went as I expected it would. The social worker gave me pamphlets full of information and resources and told me about the support the Alzheimer's Association could offer me. I knew the drill, but what I didn't realize was just how helpful things were about to become.

As I was flipping through the information, they talked a bit amongst themselves before telling me that my mother doesn't fit the profile for having Alzheimer's. I kind of agreed, but questioned why she acting the way she did. Could she somehow just be fooling everyone?

I couldn't figure it out and it appeared, as though neither could they.

"We've seen cases where the symptoms are different and your mother may just be one of the people that doesn't fit within the obvious grid," said Ted.

The social worker theorized that my mother might just have an underlying medical condition that could be temporarily causing her mental distress. She advised me to take her to a medical doctor for a full physical with blood tests and an evaluation, and if possible to get her in to see a neurologist for an MRI scan of her brain. She told me how I could prearrange everything she needs by sending the doctor information in advance and how I should be forceful about it. That sounded like a good plan. Karen handed me her card and told me to call her anytime.

I spoke to my mother about changing her Medicare provider plan to another provider in order to get a new doctor who might be able to offer her something more. During the open enrollment period towards the end of the year we found a new provider. Her new plan would become effective starting the 1st of January.

In the meantime I was interested in finding out as much as I possibly could about the aging brain. The word dementia kept popping up on all my searches. There is a wide spectrum of dementia symptoms. It's more than just a person not remembering certain events or who the President of the United States currently is. Dementia is when the brain no longer communicates with the rest of the body properly. When there is a blockage or malfunction, the brain cannot send messages to the nerves, muscles and organs for the body to respond.

Could my mother's worsening immobility, incontinence and also her increasing inability to grasp and hold things in her hands be related to dementia? And if so, what kind?

There are so many different kinds of dementia. Some related to Alzheimer's disease, some not. The only way to know for sure was to get her tested. But first, she needed to see a doctor for a full medical workup and obtain the referral needed to be seen by a neurologist.

I felt as though I was at a crossroads with my mother. The thing that helped me the most while waiting was to keep in mind that whatever the underlying cause, her obstinate and erratic be-havior was not all her fault. Realizing this made such a big differ-ence in my attitude. I have used the line "Attitude is so important" so many times while raising my own children. It was time for me to take my own advice.

My mother's health continued to decline. It was so hard for her to face the fact that she was losing more of her independence day by day. It was also hard for me, seeing this happening to her. I heard the frustration in her voice when she called out in a panic as she struggled on her bed to get into a sitting position.

Another time she trapped herself in the bathroom by backing her power chair up against the door and falling while trying to get to toilet. I can't even tell you how many times we called the para-medics to help us pick her up from the floor. We should have just given them a key to our house.

We finally took the therapist's suggestion and ordered a hospi-tal bed and a Hoyer lift. The first couple of days getting her in and out of the Hoyer lift were challenging. It was more emotional than physical as the possibility of her becoming bed ridden started to sink in. I had worked so hard, trying to keep her from getting to that point. Being bedridden would have such adverse affects on her circulation. I set the Hoyer lift aside and concentrated on help-ing her become more skillful in using the bed to help her lift her-self up. With the push of a button she was able to help herself up into a sitting position much easier. She raised and lowered the bed to lessen the pressure on her knees while transferring on and off of it. I bought her a portable exercise peddle bike and showed her how she could use it to exercise both her arms and legs. Just as long as she was willing, I wasn't going to let her go down without a fight. I accepted the fact that she wouldn't walk again, but I wasn't ready to accept her becoming permanently bedridden.

Could it be Dementia?

Help Tip:

Symptoms of dementia vary depending on the cause and the area of the brain that is affected.

General symptoms of dementia are:
- Memory loss.
- Trouble recalling events, recognizing people or places.
- Trouble finding the right words.
- Problems carrying out common tasks.
- Trouble exercising judgment.
- Not keeping up with personal care.

Certain types of dementia cause particular symptoms:
- People who have dementia with Lewy bodies have highly detailed visual hallucinations. They may fall frequently.
- Symptoms of frontotemporal dementia may experience personality or behavior changes. They say rude things, expose themselves or make sexually explicit comments.
- Symptoms of vascular dementia can be caused by a series of strokes or one that comes on suddenly.
- Delirium can appear to be dementia. Delirium is short-term confusion caused by a new or worsening illness.

Source WebMD: www.webmd.com/alzheimers/tc/dementia-symptoms

Memory loss can be caused by conditions other than dementia, such as depression and conditions that can be treated. Occasional trouble with memory (such as briefly forgetting) can be a normal part of aging. If you are worried about memory loss or if a loved one has memory loss that is getting worse, see your doctor.

Lucy (center)
with sisters Ann (left) and Barbara (right)

"Life is a storm my young friend.
You will bask in the sunlight one moment,
be shattered on the rocks the next.
What makes you a man is what
you do when that storm comes."

~Alexandre Dumas

CATEGORY 5: Hurricane

We got through the holidays and on Saturday, January 3rd I noticed how red and swollen my mother's feet had become and how blotchy her legs looked. During the day she started to complain that her right foot hurt. She also had a cough. I voiced my concerns and she agreed to go to the doctor. I tried locating a handicapped van service to transport her to the emergency room, but none where available on the weekend. So I made transportation arrangements and a doctor's appointment for her for Monday afternoon.

An hour before the bus was to pick us both up I ran to the bank while my mother sat at the dining room table finishing her lunch. When I got back 20 minutes later she was gone. My husband said she asked him to open the sliding glass door for her so she could wait for the bus outside. He didn't think anything of it and let her go. She took that opportunity to try and escape. She was successful at it to a point, as she had totally slipped out of sight. I went looking for her everywhere I could think of that she may have gone to hideout. She missed the bus and her appointment with the new doctor.

An hour later she finally called. "Elaine, I'm sorry," she said. "I'm okay. I don't want to go to the doctor's. There's nothing they can do for me," she sighed.

"Mom, you need to be seen by a doctor because you may have an infection in your foot. It's too red and swollen now. You don't want to get gangrene do you? Just tell me where you are so I can come and look at it again," I pleaded.

As soon as I hung up with her, I called Karen, the social worker at that Alzheimer's Association to tell her what had happened. She told me that it's not the ideal situation, but getting her to the hospital in the state she was currently in can be an opportunity to have some of the tests she needs done, sooner rather than later. So I called 911 and told them I was worried about her and where she was.

As it turns out, I didn't have to be the one to make that call. When I arrived, two police cars along with a fire truck and an ambulance were there. An officer on the scene told me he witnessed a confused woman crossing against a red light and called it in. The paramedics were talking to her.

"What happened?" I asked.

"I was afraid this was going to happen. I had trouble crossing the street," my mother confessed.

Whew...I was off the hook.

The patience the paramedics showed examining her and having her answer certain questions in an attempt to help her talk herself into going to the hospital couldn't have been better. Once they got her into the ambulance I was able to park her scooter in one of the stores nearby. I rode in the ambulance with her and called my husband to pick up the car.

She became very impatient while waiting to be seen. Finally a doctor came in to say that she would need to be admitted to treat the infection in her foot and that they wanted to run some further tests regarding how swollen her hands, feet and legs were.

She went ballistic. There was no way I was going to take her back home in the condition she was in and also miss the window of opportunity to find out if doctors at the hospital would begin the process of evaluating her mental state while she was there.

Once they admitted her she was diagnosed her as having congestive heart failure. OMG. I did not want to hear those words. I knew first hand how serious congestive heart failure could be as both her mother and sister had succumbed to it. The doctor saw how upset and worried I was and tried to reassure me that people can live years having congestive heart failure.

"It can be managed," he said.

He went on to explain that my mother's heart is weak from the strain it has been under trying to pump the backed up fluid in her system. I'd like to put her on a diuretic to help her release the fluid and an antibiotic to treat the infection in her foot, but she's not being cooperative.

I was so glad I hadn't caved in when she went ballistic about being admitted. She was right where she needed to be as far as I was concerned. I stayed with her during the day and went home at night to get some much needed uninterrupted sleep.

When I arrived the following morning the nurse pulled me aside to tell me that she had a bad night and the doctor put in a request for psychiatry to see her sometime that day.

My mother pleaded with me to get her out of there. I told her I couldn't take care of her while she was still so sick and that she needed to stay in the hospital in order to get well.

She ranted and raved about all the crazy things she said she saw going on during the night. The tales she told were bazaar. She insisted she wasn't safe there and that now she was so sorry for saying all the nasty things she had said about me during the night. She went on to say that she would fix it so I wouldn't get in any trouble. I didn't even want to know what she might have said. I just told her not to worry about it and that everything would be okay.

Her breakfast was still sitting on the tray. She told me she couldn't eat because the food they served the old people was laced with poison. As soon as lunch arrived I showed her how I wasn't afraid to eat the food they served. She reluctantly shared a few bites with me. She then asked me to go down to the cafeteria and bring her up something that she might like better. At least she was getting some food in her system that way.

A doctor from the psychiatry department came in to talk to her. I sat there in awe; amazed at the way my mother was able to turn "the crazy" (manipulative paranoia) on and off at the drop of a hat. She was able to carry on a conversation and answered all the questions the psychiatrist asked her so precisely. I was pretty sure that the psychiatrist was on to her though. She said everything too perfectly. I walked with the psychiatrist out into the corridor where she told me that my mother was suffering from paranoia, most likely brought on by illness. Due to her age she wasn't ruling out dementia but it was something that they would address once she was well. She also said she could prescribe a mild drug that would help with the paranoia. Since my mother had finally agreed to take the diuretic and the antibiotic the other doctor ordered, I said it was worth a try. I 'm not sure if they needed her permission before giving her the drug, but the following morning when I walked into her hospital room she appeared to be all doped up.

Was this the way she was going to be from now on by taking that drug? I was not pleased at all about having my mother end up turning into a zombie. I told the doctor I wanted her off of it immediately and preferred to wait to get her properly tested before giving her any other drugs like that again.

Everything she was unnecessarily putting herself through took such a toll on her body. I called my cousin Mary to ask her if she thought my mother might be better off being transferred to the hospital she works at. Mary said it would be better to keep her where she was, in a hospital close by, in case she needed anything right away. The hospital she worked in was an hour and a half away.

Mary then said she would try to talk some sense into her over the phone, so I handed the phone to my mother. Mary reassured her aunt that she was receiving the best of care in the hospital where she was, answered all my mother's questions and addressed her concerns.

Finally, by the fourth day my mother seemed better. Her foot wasn't as red and the swelling had gone way down. She still had a persistent cough, but it was loosening up.

I asked the nurse if they could start getting her up and moving again. I told just a little fib about her being able to walk a very short distance. It took three people to help her get up onto her feet holding on to a walker with a gait belt being held around her waist. She walked five "shuffling" steps to the chair and eased her down into a sitting position on the chair. That little bit of effort, exhausted her. After catching her breath she excitedly exclaimed, I did it," followed by a big sigh.

Witnessing how well she was starting to respond to the help and care she was receiving warmed my heart. As she sat up in the chair, willingly eating the lunch they served that day, I noticed how her sense of spirit was returning.

For such a long time it had become increasingly difficult for my husband and I to handle caring for her at home. My husband was great about helping me with some of the shifting and lifting to reposition her in bed when she'd slide down too far to help herself. He was also good at being willing to keep an eye on her so I could go to the grocery store or take a quick walk around the block to get a breath of fresh air. The brunt of the burden to bath her, change her, cook for all of us, clean and keep our house sanitized was solely on my shoulders.

My whole family was concerned about me. They wanted me to stop killing myself by either hiring help or putting her where they felt she belonged, in a nursing home. I had hired an agency once but I didn't feel that I got the help I truly needed. I too was at the point of wanting to break the promise I had made my mother of never putting her in a nursing home. Well, sort of.

What I really wanted was for her to "get a life" again. I wanted her to socialize and be kept entertained. I wanted her to become motivated and involved in activities that she could take pleasure in doing. I had to face the fact that she had slowed down quite a bit and it wasn't convenient for her to participate in activities outside of the house anymore. Perhaps being in a well-run active assisted living place might really be good for her. But, what I didn't want was for her to feel trapped in a facility or in a place where she would have to see zombie-like drugged up old people sitting in wheelchairs in hallways.

I called the Age Well senior services agency in our area to inquire about what might be available nearby. They referred me to Dorothy Carter a senior care placement coordinator. Dorothy suggested that my mother might be better off going into a more family oriented board and care home. We then talked about pricing. There was no way my mother would be able to afford it, even if we pitched in a little bit too. So she suggested I call Kristy

O'Brien regarding a VA benefit my mother might qualify for that could help with the cost.

So I called Kristy at the War Era Veterans Alliance to find out about it. Kristy explained that the VA benefit is called "The Improved Pension Aid and Attendance Entitlement Fund." My father having served in the military during wartime and being married to my mother at the time of his death qualified my mother for this benefit. All my mother would have to do is provide the proper paperwork needed to apply for this benefit in order to receive the full spousal amount of $1049.00 a month. Using that along with her social security check every month would cover most of the cost for living in a board and care home.

The War Era Veterans Alliance Kristy works for is a non-profit organization. She walked me through the entire process and helped me submit the application. If you'd like to talked to Kristy regarding this benefit feel free to contact her calling or writing to:

War Era Veterans Alliance
120 Vantis, Suite 300
Aliso Viejo, CA 92656,
949-207-7780
www.WarEraVet.com
Contact Person: Kristy O'Brien

The following day Dorothy took me to see a board and care home that seemed like a good fit for my mother. What sold me on this particular home was, the owner Sandy and her husband Ed, treat all the residents like family. The couple ran a small four-bed board and care home in their own home. They have one full time live-in caregiver and Sandy said her adult-children come over often to help out too. During our tour I couldn't help but notice several photographs throughout the house, which gave me the impression that they must be a close-knit family. Sandy also happened to mention that her grandkids visit often.

"Perfect," I thought. I told her how much my mother would enjoy her grandkids and asked if I could take some photos of her home with my camera to show my mother. She said sure, and also lent me a couple of photographs of the residents with her grandkids to show my mother.

The couple said they'd make room for my mother's lift chair in the den along with hooking up the hearing device my mother used while watching TV. I liked the large room my mother would share with another lady and loved that it had a sliding glass door leading out into the backyard where there was a garden and a heated pool. Sandy also said she encourages family to come over anytime.

"Mi casa es su casa," she said.

The only drawback was they didn't allow power chairs or scooters in the house. My mother could use hers outdoors only. Indoors my mother could either walk with a walker or she would be wheeled around in a transport wheelchair that they would provide. Well, I certainly didn't want her to be stuck in a wheelchair all day, but in the back of my mind I thought that maybe not having her power chair might actually motivate her to try and walk again. She'd be able to get some physical therapy for a while. I just wasn't sure how successful she'd be at it. But it was worth a shot.

I had all the information I needed, but it was not a decision I was going to make for her by myself. I returned to the hospital to talk to her about it and show her the photos. Surprisingly my mother seemed very excited about moving there.

"I've been feeling like we need to give each other some space," she said. She went on to say, "I don't like keeping you from living your own life. I want you to be able to go out anytime you want and take the trips you talk about taking with Mike."

We also talked about some of the things she wanted to do to live a better life. During our conversation I was impressed by how clear she was regarding some of the mistakes she admitted to having made in her life. I told her that I didn't want her to ever feel as though I wanted to just get rid of her. I let her know that I was hoping this new arrangement would bring us closer together.

Tears were streaming down my face as I said, "All I've ever wanted was for you and I to be able to live the kind of lives we both deserved."

I had felt sorry for my mother throughout my whole life. Through my childhood eyes, I saw my mother as being such a strong willed, powerful, yet lonely woman. I saw how she pushed her way into opportunities that were not hers for the taking. She relied solely on her family for whatever happiness she could squeeze out of them for herself. My mother had a lot of talent, gumption, and such an entrepreneurial spirit that could have taken her far in life. She was just too afraid and insecure to step out of her comfort zone to take leaps of faith on her own. Everything she accomplished, she accomplished within the walls of her own home.

During my teenager years, I remember how much she had wanted to purchase a beautiful four-plex she saw for sale that was right across the street from the park. She saw the income potential that owning that property would provide. She also mentioned wanting to one day buy a large home she could turn into a bed and breakfast. She had ideas, lots of ideas. She also had problems. She was a food-a-holic. The obsession she had about needing to constantly talk about food used to drive me crazy. Everyone has faults, but the most important thing my mother had was heart.

We talked more that afternoon than we had ever talked like that together before. My mother liked to talk and I was sure she'd have the opportunity to get the attention she craved by talking to the ladies at Sandy's board and care home.

My mother being willing to give me my freedom, felt like a gift. The burden of responsibility for her care that would be lifted off my shoulders would be huge. Not being under so much stress would also open the door to having more time to spend quality time with her when I visited. I'd take her out to lunch and maybe shopping too. Yes, I'd visit often.

The following afternoon the doctor was ready to release her.

"But, she has still has a cough," I said feeling as though the timing was all wrong for her to be leaving so soon.

My husband and I needed time to move her things into the board and care home she would be going directly to. I wanted to get everything set up for her ahead of time. Plus it would be better if she left in the morning so she would have a full day to adjust to her new surroundings before I had to leave in the evening.

Finally, the doctor said that under the circumstances he would extend her stay in the hospital for one more day.

My mother had a fit and all hell broke loose. She insisted on leaving that night. Different doctors and nurses kept coming in to take her blood pressure, draw blood, and try to get her to agree to the MRI scan she hadn't yet agree to. She screamed at all the technicians to get the hell out and for me to get her out of there before they kill her. She was hysterical.

While I was on the phone with a transportation company to arrange for a wheelchair van, Sandy walked in the door and into all the chaos. I had no idea she had been called.

My mother calmed down a bit as Sandy told her how much the other ladies were looking forward to welcoming her to the family.

Then, a nurse came in to hand Sandy my mother's release papers. The moment that happened, my mother became terrified again. I think in her mind she had rationalized that Sandy was in cahoots with the hospital. I believe she thought that the hospital was afraid to kill her because she was too loud. Instead the new plan they arranged was to dispose of her by taking her to Sandy's house so they could get away with it in a quieter way. She kept shifting her eyes back and forth from the doctor to the nurse to Sandy and then to me as if indicating for me to pay attention to what she was sure she had figured out was going on.

She mouthed these words to me, "This is murder. What you are doing is murdering your mother." She mouthed with squinted her eyes of such conviction.

"Get me out of here," she started to scream again.

"Don't worry about it. Your mother will be fine at our house. We have been in the caregiving business for over eighteen years, and have dealt with many difficult cases. Please, just make sure to bring her medication," Sandy said with a reassuring tone to her voice.

"Medication? What medication?" I thought to myself.

The only prescription medication she would be taking is a heart pill and a diuretic as needed to help her release any reoccurring fluid. We weren't going to consider any other medications until after receiving a proper diagnosis.

I am not an advocate for medications. Neither is my mother and certainly not medications that only serve to put a Band-Aid on a problem. In my opinion, only when a person is in serious danger should the quickest temporary relief be through the pharmacy door until a more permanent solution can be determined. My mother might be in serious trouble but she isn't in danger by not taking a zombie medication. I'm sorry if dealing with her was going to be unnerving until then, but I wasn't willing to have her medicated just to make it easier for someone else.

A nurse wheeled my mother downstairs once she was released. Things went from bad to worse. The transportation service I arranged for sent the wrong van, which my mother didn't recognize as being the transportation she usually takes. As they were wheeling her into the big bright yellow taxi van I heard her say under her breath, "I cooked my own goose this time."

On the ride to Sandy's house, she started to shake her head violently as if going into a seizure, which she wasn't. I asked her what was wrong she said she couldn't talk about it. That it was too horrible to say.

"What do you mean?" I responded.

She pleaded with me not to take her to Sandy's house. She repeated over and over again, "Please, please don't do this to me. I can't go there. They will kill me tonight. Please don't do this to me." She repeated it over and over.

I couldn't take it anymore. I gave the driver my home address and asked him to please just take us both home instead. She looked outside the window to make sure the driver was going the right way. I felt relieved, but for other reasons than hers. I didn't really feel comfortable leaving her in a strange place while she was still so sick. Her persistent coughing concerned me. The social worker had warned me that transition from the hospital goes a lot smoother than making the transition from home. That was the farthest thing from my mind at the time. I felt that bringing her home for a few days would give her the extra time she needed to recuperate from her illness and from the ordeal she had gone through while at the hospital. At that particular time, I felt it would be in her best interest to take everything one step at a time.

Pitfalls to Patience

Help Tip:

Have you noticed how fast our society moves? We eat at fast food restaurants and buy ready-made food at the grocery store. We drive 70 mph on freeways and pay tolls electronically via "Fast Track." We watch movies at home "on demand" and at Disneyland, the "happiest place on earth," we purchase a "Fast Pass" to avoid waiting in long lines.

This super fast-paced world isn't one that most elderly people can keep up with. As caregivers we should shift into a lower gear and embrace the character trait of patience. Patience requires empathy by being willing to walk in step with another.

How-to tips to develop more patience:

- **Practice delaying gratification.**
  If you can't live without what you impulsively want to buy at least wait a day before going back to purchase it.

- **Remind yourself that things take time.**
  Impatient people tend to forget that some things just can't be rushed. Almost anything really good in life takes time and dedication. By being too impatient you may become too eager to give up on relationships, goals and other things that are important to you.

- **Give yourself a break.**
  Take a few minutes to do absolutely nothing. Just sit quietly and think. Don't watch TV or read. Just do nothing. It may be hard at first, but slowing your world down, is a good way of developing the attitude necessary to have more patience.

*"It is not your job to save everyone.
Some people are not even ready to be helped.
Focus on being of service to those who are
And be wise and humble enough to know
when the best service you can offer is to
guide them toward help in another direction."*

~Ann Taylor

CHAPTER 4

AFTERMATH

Once home, I knew I made the right choice. Over the next few days the coughing had subsided, but her feet were swelling up again and her arms and legs were weeping: a term that's used when fluid leaks through the skin. The bottoms of her feet also looked blue, especially when they weren't being raised. This worried me. Her voice had also changed to where she sounded like she was getting out of breath. She insisted she wasn't getting out of breath, she just felt weak. From what I know about congestive heart failure I was pretty sure her condition had progressed to Stage 4.

My mother refused home health care. The on-call doctor assigned to her, instructed me to double the dosage on the diuretic she was taking to help reduce the strain that was being placed on her heart from the excess fluid build up in her system. She prescribed a potassium supplement that she suggested she take with it, as the fluid being released by taking the diuretic would deplete her potassium levels. She refused to take the potassium supplement. We resolved that issue by giving her potassium rich bananas and potatoes instead.

I brushed her body with a soft brush twice a day to stimulate her circulation and help her lymphatic system get moving. Slowly but surely the swelling finally went way down.

She seemed to be on the mend again.

Some days she had a better appetite than other days. I never forced my mother to eat but I encouraged her by spoon-feeding her nutritious, easy to eat foods as often as I could.

She enjoyed the homemade Greek yogurt cheesecakes I made her topped with fruit and whipped cashew cream.

She also liked the fresh vegetable juices and smoothies I gave her to sip throughout the day. I usually slipped an avocado and some high protein hemp seeds into her smoothies, and sometimes super-foods such as Maca powder, Spirulina and Chlorella.

She was sleeping a little better during the night, and started to eat more on her own.

My husband and I moved some of the furniture around in our house to make it easier for us to move her from her bedroom, into the living room by using the Hoyer lift again so she wouldn't be confined to her bedroom. We had a pretty good handle on the situation by then and my mother had jumped over yet another hurdle.

My mother and I had taken some detours and gotten terribly lost. But we were able to find our way back to restoring the damage we had both caused. In the process, we discovered a special mother/daughter bond that we probably had all along. Sure, there were things that could have been done better. Becoming aware was the first step toward making a plan to change.

As difficult as this situation was for all of us I believe that caring for my mother in our home was the right thing to do. Of all the things my mother has ever had a hand in teaching me the lessons I have learned while navigating through this storm with her I believe were the most important ones.

*"In times of grief and sorrow I will hold you and rock you
and take your grief and make it my own.
When you cry I cry, and when you hurt I hurt.
And together we will try to hold back the floods of tears
and despair and make it through the potholed streets of life."*

~ Nicholas Sparks, The Notebook

My mother always had something going for her. She was of the mindset that "prescription medications don't cure what ails you." I think that's a major factor as to why she lived so long. I too have that same belief to a certain extent. I am just not as stubborn as she is about it. I believe that there are times when the body needs a little extra help to get over the hump when there is a medical emergency.

I think my mother's paranoia; feeling as though everyone was out to get her, was in conflict with her logic. She lived such a fearful life. She would literally spend hours reading the contradictions of medications trying to figure out whether or not she should take what the doctor prescribed. She used to call "Joe" the pharmacist in Las Vegas, to get his opinion on a certain medication. It's good to be cautious, but she took it to the extreme.

It's true that all medications have side affects. A lot of times a second medication is prescribed to alleviate the side affects of the first one, etc. It can become a vicious circle. The issue with my mother was that she didn't seem to comprehend when the positives outweighed the negatives when it came to medications.

I can understand how older people may feel as though they are easy prey. There's a pill for everything and a lot of seniors end up becoming overly medicated. It has become a big problem in our society.

I've also heard that doctors receive perks and are often encouraged by the pharmaceutical industry to fill sales quotas. There are good doctors out there though. I respect them for their integrity of upholding the oath they took to, "First, do no harm." After all, the father of medicine, Hippocrates said, "Let food be thy medicine, and medicine be thy food."

I lost focus and relied on the health care system's help for my mother for a long time. In a way I fell prey to trying to get my mother as much care as she was qualified to receive, even though time after time after time I saw that she wasn't getting the kind of care that she truly needed from the medical profession in the name of Medicare benefits. It's not the doctors' fault. I realized how doctor's hands were tied in a lot of ways. In my opinion, the medical profession isn't put in the position to treat old age. Doctors are trained to medicate disease.

I'm very sorry to say that the health care system was willing to pay to help my mother die by offering her round the clock Hospice services, but they were not willing to pay for her to live by offering to go the distance with her for the kind of care and rehabilitation she truly needed to improve the quality of her life. What's wrong with this picture?

The home health care my mother received was always temporary. Like the therapist told me, "they are not maintenance people." But that is what people like my mother need. My mother needed "maintenance people," working with her long enough to help her get stronger and give her a chance to improve to the point of not needing so much help. How can you put a time limit on that? Most elderly people are not able to continue improving solely on their own, certainly not as quickly as they are expected to. That extra burden of responsibility also gets dumped right on the caregivers lap, as if they don't have enough to do already.

After feeling as though the health care system had failed my mother I knocked on the doors of every organization that I could think of, to try and get some help for her and for myself. By this time I was drowning too. I was at the point where my own health was in jeopardy.

I know what caregivers go through because I went through it myself. There was very little help available to me. I searched endlessly, which was exhausting. Caregivers don't have the energy or the time to go the distance like that. And still I came up short. I couldn't believe that there were so many agencies, yet no affordable help available.

I found out about the Aid and Attendance VA Entitlement benefit my mother qualified for too late. She could have been receiving that $1,049.00 a month for at least the past ten years if we had known about it sooner. Entitled. Who's entitled? How can you be entitled to something you aren't told you are entitled too?

If we had known about that benefit when she was still living in Las Vegas they could have used it to get someone in to stay with her while Sara was at work. Even just a few hours a day would have helped a lot.

There are so many elderly people in the same boat as my mother was. They are barely scrapping by with what little money they receive from their monthly social security check. My mother was able to rely on living with her family for housing. There was no way my mother could afford to pay for rent, utilities and food if she would have been able to live on her own. The money some of these seniors may have in the bank will either all go to pay for their elderly care or it will end up being used for the out of pocket medical bills that Medicare doesn't cover. There may or may not then be enough left over for their final expenses. Otherwise guess who gets the bill, their children.

There are quite a few agencies that offer support groups for caregivers. I'm fortunate that my husband was willing to stay with my mother so that I could go a couple of times, but what about the caregivers that need it the most but can't get to the support groups because it's either too difficult to find someone to stay with their loved one or if allowed it's too difficult to bring them, especially if their loved one is wheelchair bound.

I looked into getting my mother into an adult day care once. I thought giving her the opportunity to socialize more would be good for her. I even talked to the director to see if they would agree to let my mother "think" she was just a volunteer there, which they said they would. But, it was very expensive and most of the people that are able to attend qualify through receiving the low income Medicaid benefit. In order to qualify for Medicaid (which is referred to as Medical in California) they have to be practically destitute.

Agencies that offer volunteer services are great. In fact I am sure most volunteers would go way beyond the call of duty if they could because that's the kind of people they are. But their hands are tied too because of rules they too must abide by. Agencies told me that volunteers are only qualified to be gophers and companions. They are not allowed to change a diaper, bathe a person and in some instances they aren't even allowed to comb another person's hair. A volunteer can go to the grocery store for you, be there as a companion to talk to your loved one, play a game, or read to them, all of which are much needed, very appreciated help and support. The problem is, there's usually a very long waiting list before a volunteer becomes available. It's almost like you have to put your parent on the list years before you need the help so their name appears closer to the top by the time you need them. Who can possibly plan ahead like that?

I could go on and on about the help caregivers need and don't get. I think what society doesn't seem to "get" is that caregivers are dealing with loved ones that in most cases aren't able to help themselves, that's why they need assistance and care. I "get" it. It's way beyond a full time job: it's 24/7. To put it bluntly, it's life sucking. In most instances caregivers give up a huge chunk of their life by being a caregiver. And they lovingly do so. It just saddens me to know that so many caregivers; in fact 60% or more, end up becoming ill or dying because it's all too much to handle on their own.

I took that as a big wake up call to stop searching for information and answers within the health care system. I am fortunate that I was able to stop the madness and get a better handle on working out the kinks to relieve all the stress I had been under.

I still did all the same things that I had been doing to care for my mother's basic daily needs. As her caregiver, that did not change. What changed was I started to put my oxygen mask on first. By putting my own oxygen mask on first, I felt more important and so did my mother, because I was then able to give her better, less stressful care. It's amazing how being an important person erases abusive behavior. By taking better care of myself, I was able to begin to care for my mother without sacrificing my own health and wellbeing. That was the way it should have been from the beginning.

Everyone deserves to live the kind of life they can live to the best of their ability without ownership, burden or infringement on another person's life.

I underestimated how simply spending time with my mother was healing for the both of us. I was able to stop the madness and take the opportunity to tell my mother I recognized all she had done for me, and how much I appreciated all she had done for my family as well. She deserved to hear that from me.

I took the time to have tea with her. She told me stories about her past that I loved hearing more about. I found it fascinating that the positive memories we had shared overshadowed the negatives. The negatives just weren't as important anymore because we took the time to understand each other better by communicating more. It also had everything to do with simply deciding to forgive each other's faults.

I feel fortunate that my husband had always supported my decision to care for my mother in our home. He deserves a lot of credit for all he has endured and for all the help he has given me. I'm glad he didn't take things my mother said as personally as I did sometimes. He was able to find humor in and accept a lot of my mother's oddities. He was the one who would take a different course of action than I did at first. He'd go out to buy earplugs whereas I wanted to solve the mystery behind why my mother babbled on and on some days like a broken record playing in the background of her mind.

And so you learn. You learn what each other's strengths and weaknesses are and you work together to make it happen. We mostly worked on setting boundaries. When I brought up the subject of setting some limits my mother threw me for a loop when she confronted me by indicating that I had still not been as communicative as I should have been with her. Touché. She questioned where my nastiness went and why I was being so nice all of a sudden. Changing too quickly made her become suspicious that something else was going on that I wasn't telling her about. So, lesson learned.

At times my mother's stubbornness threw everything off, but that's the thing with an aging parent, their behavior can be unpredictable.

My mother had been very sick, probably for far longer than anyone knew. The things I was doing for her were helping, but I couldn't manage to get the synergy of care she needed.

Some days were better than others. Some days she was able to get up and about for a while in her scooter or power chair, other days she was not. Some days she sounded more like her self again, other days not so much. Some days her feet and legs look back to normal, other days they look like they were starting to swell again. Some days she would say she wanted to go out to lunch, other days she wanted to just go back to bed. She was very alert most of the time, but tired easily.

There was one thing she was very persistent in doing. She talked incessantly about a movie that was playing in her head.

She would say, "There's a movie being made, and terrible things are happening. I don't want the mafia to make the movie. I need to stop it from being made before they have a chance to finish it."

She'd get the details in the movie mixed up sometimes, but the premise was always the same. The movie that was being made was a horrible one whereby she and others were in danger if these mafia type people weren't stopped in time. We tried to ease her concern by telling her that she was safe, we were safe and everyone in the family was safe and no one was in danger. We even told her that we were able to stop the movie from being made, but she wouldn't believe us. Our children also tried talking to her to no avail. This movie was stuck in her head and it kept playing over and over again.

When we couldn't convince her otherwise I sought out help from the mental health department. The only way I felt I would possibly be able to get her to go to the appointment was by telling her that it was for me. I told her if she came with me we would go out to lunch afterwards, otherwise she would be staying home alone since my husband Mike would not be home to stay with her that day.

During the appointment, she disclosed that her father had a hard time controlling his temper. She said she was sorry that this trait had been passed down to others in the family. While the therapist was probing her for further explanation, my mother turned to me and said, "What does this all have to do with your appointment, Elaine?" She was on to me. I played it cool by telling her that she was saying things that were helping me. The conversation shifted.

"You don't tell me everything that's going on," she complained. "I know someone is in trouble. You should never have tricked me into coming here. I know what you are trying to do," she scolded.

She was done. It took me a minute to think about what my response should be and luckily the therapist stepped in before I could say anything.

"It is very common to lash out and hurt the ones you love the most and feel the safest with," she explained.

After the appointment I lagged behind so the therapist could tell me what the next step should be, "Your mother's problems run deep, but at her age she may not benefit from the standard goal setting therapy sessions that we offer. What I can offer you is to see her on a temporary basis to act only as a sounding board for her whenever she needs to talk to get things off her chest." The therapist also mentioned that a psychiatrist could prescribe a medication to help with the paranoia.

On the bus ride home I lightened the mood by mentioning that we could take a trip to Las Vegas to visit Sophie and her new little baby sister Amy, whom we hadn't seen yet. She liked that idea. We decided to wait and take that trip the following month when Sara's sister Marlene would also be visiting. This way we'd also be able to see Marlene's new baby boy Richie Jr., named after his father Richard.

There weren't many things my mother was frivolous about spending money on, except when it came to buying airline tickets and getting her nails done. She could care less about going to the beauty salon to have her hair washed, set and curled, but she just loved pretty nails. Out of the blue one day, a couple of weeks later she wanted to go get her nails done. I walked beside her as she rode her scooter down to the beauty parlor. While she was getting her nails done, I ran across the street to pick up a few groceries.

The following the day my mother slept on and off while sitting in her chair in the living room. I asked her if she wanted me to go to the library to get her some books to read and she said, no that her eyes were bothering her. The last time I had taken her to see an optometrist he indicated that she was starting to show signs of cataracts and referred her to an ophthalmologist. Oh course she didn't want to go. She was concerned about her eyes and often put eye drops in them, but needed time to think about whether or not she wanted to have the cataract surgery.

I simply said, "I'll make you carrot juice for your eyes in the meantime."

When she wasn't dosing on and off in the living room chair during the day, she was sitting there talking about that dang movie that continued to play in her head. That night she wouldn't let me help her into bed. She insisted on sitting up in her living room chair all night. I didn't dim the lights that night. I kept them on so she could keep watch, like she wanted to. However I did turn the TV off. I couldn't trust that a program might come on that would be too violent for her to be watching.

Our family came over the following day to celebrate my birthday on Monday, February 2nd. She came to the table to eat dinner with us, but she couldn't seem to engage in conversation. She started to talk about the movie to everyone at the table and it became a little freaky. Our son Benjamin stuck around after the party. He sat with her for over an hour talking to her hoping to offer her whatever help he could to ease her mind from whatever was bothering her. My mother was very receptive as they talked while our son listened for clues in an attempt to make sense of it all. They happened to get on the subject of books and he mentioned that there is one particular book that he likes that she might also like. She said she'd like to read it and he brought the book over the following day.

She was calm and agreeable when I helped her into bed after our son left that evening. The following morning she wasn't interested in getting out of bed to go into the living room. I understood how tired she was from having stayed up all night the night before. She obviously needed her rest and I let her slept most of that day.

Healthy Boundaries

Help Tip:

Good boundaries let us maintain an emotional bond of love, concern, and caring without the negative results of desperation, rescuing, enabling, fixing, or controlling. By respecting each other's boundaries, you show respect for each other. In most instances it's you, the caregiver who needs to set your own limits. At times their stubbornness and unpredictable behavior can throw everything off. There are no written rules as to what is realistic or unrealistic. Often, you won't even know when enough is enough until the line has already been crossed. Consider this:

- **You can't do it all even though you may think you should.**
  It's hard to say no to an ill parent with diminished abilities without feeling guilty. You are not responsible for their happiness.

- **Only you can determine what you can and cannot handle.**
  You aren't being neglectful if you don't fulfill all of your parent's wants and needs. Decide when too much is too much.

- **Trust your instincts for what will work for you.**
  The better you know yourself, the clearer it will become to determine where you need to strengthen your boundaries.

- **Accept and respect.**
  When you accept and respect the boundaries of others you'll feel better about setting and upholding your own.

- **Set healthy boundaries for yourself and only yourself.**
  Value your feelings and know that you are worth it.

*"Let today be the day
that you learn the grace
of letting go
and the power
of moving on."*

~Steve Maraboli

CHAPTER 5

CLEAR SKIES

My mother passed away peacefully ten days prior to the trip to Las Vegas, we had planned to take together. Days preceding her death were quiet ones. She didn't want to leave her bedroom. She only wanted to sleep. I went in several times a day to wake her, offer her a few bites of food and give her sips of water. I sat with her, held her hand, stroked her hair, changed her position and told her all the things I thought she'd want to hear. As I sat there and talked, all the good things that she had accomplished in her life came flowing out of my mouth.

I knew she was listening because when I released my hand from hers she'd shake hers in an attempt to search for mine again. I told her to wake up. I kept repeating, "Everybody loves Grandma Lucy," and I taped photographs of family along the wall so she could see all the people that love her. I didn't call anyone but my daughter because I didn't feel up to it and I'm sure neither did she. My daughter said she would arrange to fly out the following Monday. I told her that her grandma might pass away before then. My daughter then told me something that I will never forget. "I am not coming to see or say goodbye to grandma, I am coming for you. You are the one who needs me now. I want to be there for you."

I am sure the rest of the family would have all loved to say their goodbyes to their: sister, aunt and grandmother, but I couldn't make the calls to make that happen for them. All the commotion would have been too much for both of us. Her wish, when the time came, was to go as peacefully as possible. I didn't believe the chaos of emotions by having her family around would be considered peaceful for her. She was my main concern, at the time. I am sorry if my making that decision for her has offended anyone, but I did what I felt was the right thing to do for my mother.

At night, I sat beside her bed reading her the book my son Benjamin had lent her. The short stories it contained were all such meaningful ones. They gave me something to ponder as I sat beside her. My mother was a woman who loved knowing that things served a purpose. She seemed to thrive on it. I suppose that is why she got so much joy out of teaching children how to make purposeful things out of solid wood that would last such a long time.

Two days before she passed away, she refused to open her mouth for water. She clenched it tight. We had gotten up to page fifty in the book I read to her. The following day, she threw up quite a bit of brown colored liquid. It took me a long time to clean up the mess. It was a struggle for me to move her from side to side to remove the soiled bed sheets beneath her, change her nightgown and put new linens on her bed. She resisted as I moved her back and forth. She was awake but not as responsive as she had been the day before. I moved her onto her side so she'd be able to easily spit out any more liquid if she needed to and placed a towel underneath her jaw. I wanted her to drink a little water to put a fresh taste in her mouth. She refused, so I took a washcloth and gently did it anyway.

The week before, my husband told me about an article he read on the Internet regarding the dying process. He suggested I read it because he thought she was showing quite a few of the signs. I wasn't ready to read it. I was too busy trying to keep my mother alive.

"I'll save it for you on my computer," he said.

After she refused water I knew I needed to know what to expect. I didn't want her to be in any pain. Not knowing what to expect had made me feel too ill-equipped.

I was also mad. Mad at the fact that she had left this all up to me to try and figure out myself. It might have been more comforting to all of us if she would have allowed me to call for hospice services. They may have been able to provide her with comfort care. Luckily she was not in any discomfort that I could tell. I could have called hospice then, but what if it wasn't the end? *What if, what if, what if...* I didn't want to make that call, because if I did, it would mean that I had resigned by giving up all hope. I couldn't do that to her. Instead, I went to my husband's computer and read the article he had saved for me and to read through the ten signs death is near list.

Ten Signs death is near

1. Loss of appetite
2. Excessive fatigue and sleep
3. Increased physical weakness
4. Mental confusion or disorientation
5. Labored breathing
6. Social withdrawal
7. Changes in urination
8. Swelling in the feet and ankles
9. Coolness in the tips of the fingers and toes
10. Mottled veins

Author Paula Spencer Scoot, goes into great detail regarding each of these warning signs.

Source Caring.com: www.caring.com/articles/signs-of-death

I knew my mother didn't want any medical intervention when the time came. We had talked about her wishes on and off over the course of the last several years. She didn't like talking about it, but I wanted to know what she would want. So I'd ask her a question here and there to find out. The last time she was in the hospital, we talked again. She agreed a DNR (Do Not Resuscitate) order should be in place, but she didn't want to be the one to sign it. She just wanted it to be known that it was her wish. My mother didn't like signing any legal documents of any kind.

Her doctor told me that without a signed DNR in her records she would not have a choice. Knowing her wishes I signed the paperwork the doctor filled out to assign me as the person to make medical decisions on her behalf since she had expressed that wish in front of both of us.

My mother also did not want to be kept alive by having anything shoved down her throat or hooked up to a machine. Her wishes were to pass away at home as peacefully and unobtrusively as possible. She wished to be cremated with her ashes scattered on top of her parents' graves.

She said, "I want to go back where I came from and I don't want anyone to wear black at my funeral. I want my funeral to be a celebration of my life."

August 1, 1922 – February 7, 2015

She was never interested in making any pre-arrangements, and I never pushed the issue. She kept money for her final expenses in a special fund that I had access to. And that was that. She said I'd know what to do when the time came to handle everything.

The night before my mother passed away, I stayed up into the wee hours of the morning on my computer finding solace in the writing I was doing. I could hear her labored breathing in the distance. I went into her bedroom several times throughout the night to check on her. She was sleeping peacefully. I sat beside her bed holding her hand for a while, kissed her and told her how much I loved her, and again repeated several times, "Everyone loves Grandma Lucy," as I felt that's what she wanted to hear.

I let her know that I would take care of everything for her if she wanted to go. I spoke softly, with a reassuring tone in my voice as I told her, "Everyone is okay. No one is in danger here."

I told her that her mother and father would be waiting for her, and that her great granddaughter Phoenix wanted to play with her. I told her I wanted her and Phoenix to have a tea party together, and to not forget to show her how to curl her little pinky finger up as she held the teacup to sip her tea. I also told her that her sister had been looking for her with her books in her hand.

I left the room at 1:42am to return to the kitchen table where I had left my laptop computer. At 1:45am, just moments after I sat down, I felt a silence. I jumped up and rushed back to her room to check her breathing. I couldn't feel her pulse or any air coming from her mouth. Her chest was not moving, her hands were warm and honestly, I still wasn't sure if she had passed away. I opened the lids of her eyes, which looked fixated somewhere else, somewhere beyond my comprehension.

Yes, that is when I knew she had passed away. I couldn't cover her face, nor will I ever silence her voice in my head. I kissed her forehead once more, told her that I'd miss her, and left the room. There was nothing more for me to do.

I believe that my mother did not want me to see her take her last breath, perhaps her wish was for me to remember the first breath of life she gave to me. For, that was the thought that crossed my mind at the time.

I recalled an article I had come across earlier that week stating, "After death, it is best to simply leave the person alone for several hours to give them time to move on."

And so I did.

I was still up at 2:30am when my husband woke up, wondering where I was. I met him by the hallway opening on his way to find me.

"I think my mother passed away," I said. "But she was still warm when I touched her. Go in and check for me to make sure," I asked him.

Why did I still need confirmation? I do not know. I just did. Reluctantly he went in her bedroom while I waited out in the hall. He came out seconds later and closed the door behind him. That confirmed to me that she was gone, as he wouldn't have closed her door otherwise. We had always left her door open during the night so we could hear her if she called.

He turned to me, and with a slight crackle in his voice said, " I put the covers over her head."

Honestly, I think he was in shock. I noticed how his eyes started to well up with tears.

"This is so weird," he said. He wanted to call 911, but I stopped him.

"No. Wait!" I exclaimed. "I want to give her time to leave. There is no way I want my mother sticking around here to haunt us if she is removed too soon," I explained.

We agreed to wait until the morning to make the call. I brought my laptop computer into our bedroom and together we looked up mortuaries. I didn't want anyone bringing her back to the hospital, for I knew she'd hate that. She also didn't want anyone performing an autopsy on her. I remember her stating, "Once I am gone, I am gone. That's it. *Finito!*" *(Italian for finished.)*

In bed unable to sleep, all of a sudden I felt a flickering, but couldn't quite make out what it was. It seemed like there was a small, bright yellow light softly hovering close to my neck trying to get my attention.

"It must be my mother," I thought.

I sensed a desire that she had for me to come with her. With my thoughts I wanted to let her know this was something she needed to do by herself. In my mind I tried to picture a very wide, bright white light and directed her to turn around and look for it.

"Fly into the light," I whispered. "I cannot go with you today. Everyone is waiting for you on the other side of the light. It's beautiful there. You will love it. It's time for you to go now."

A short while later, in my mind I heard her called back to me in a much younger sounding voice, "Elaine, look at me. I'm so young and thin now and I can walk. Look at me walking."

And I did see. I saw her just the way she looked in a picture I had seen of her taken when she was in her twenties. No more canes, walkers or electric power scooters. Thank God!

I asked her if she saw all the family members that were there.

"Yes, but I don't want to hang around with them just yet. I love the feeling of freedom I have now," she relayed to me. Then in my mind I heard her say, "Oh, by the way, Phoenix is adorable. She's ten now. She has long, black wavy hair. She loves skipping among the flowers, always trying to catch butterflies and she carries a sunflower with her everywhere she goes."

I don't know if I had gotten any sleep or not. I'm not sure if I was just dreaming all that I wanted to believe or not. All I know is, whatever was or wasn't happening, served to comforted me quite a bit.

The following morning our phones were dead.

"My mother's last hurrah!" I couldn't help but chuckle.

Seriously, we had no phone service. There we were, with a dead body in our home and no way to call anyone to tell them it was time to come for my mother. My husband looked a little perplexed, but finally found out that the problem was on the company's end after searching our phone provider's website for clues. We decided to wait until 8:00am to try again. If we still couldn't get through, our backup plan was to contact our son by messaging him through the computer to ask him to call 911 for us.

"So Mike, what are we going to tell the authorities when they come? Aren't they going to wonder why we waited so long to call?" I asked my husband.

"We'll just tell them that she died in her sleep," he replied.

My husband, children and I gathered together to plan her "Celebration of Life" memorial service. Our son Benjamin wrote the eulogy for the newspaper, which included a request to have a tree planted in her name in lew of sending flowers. The evening before the memorial service our four children got together with my husband and I to light candles in honor of their Grandma Lucy. Our youngest son stayed the night to help make corsages for all the family to wear during the services, while our daughter decorated special cupcakes, which ended up costing twice as much to make than to buy after needing different cake decorating tools and other decorations for the ones we decided would be perfect to make.

On Valentine's Day, family and friends met at the boat we had chartered. The first part of the celebration would take place at sea to scatter ¾ of her ashes. My daughter brought a large, butterfly shaped helium balloon for everyone to sign a goodbye message on. We would later release the balloon beside her parents' graves when we scatter ashes there as well, according to her wishes.

When my daughter arrived, two days after her grandma had passed away, we put a memorial book together using pictures, some Italian recipes that my mother enjoyed making, and other paper memorabilia that we were also able to stuff into it. We came across an old grocery list that she had written in the back of her address book, which we also included.

While family and friends thumbed through the book as we sailed out to sea, they shared the stories they said she would be remembered for the most.

Her nephew Barry recalled how fabulous the Italian cream puffs she used to make were, as his wife copied the recipe from the memorial book.

Our daughter told the chicken story about how her Grandma Lucy wanted to cater her wedding. She had bought a ton of chickens that she wanted to cook. Only problem was, there would be nowhere to store all these chickens before the wedding, nor would there be time for her grandma to prepare all of them herself for all the guests that were attending the wedding. We finally were able to get her to reconsider and hired a caterer. We ended up eating chicken dinners for months afterwards.

The funniest one she shared was the story about when we tried to teach my mother how to use her new iPhone. Our daughter had us all busting up with laughter, through our tears, as she told that one.

I didn't tell this story at the time, but the one I will never forget is when my mother helped us put up an above the ground twenty-foot round pool in our backyard. It was our son Jason's sixth birthday. We had gotten the pool's sides and top support railings up, the liner in place and the pool filled almost three-quarters of the way to the top. I left for a short time to drop off ice cream pops for the party in Jason's classroom. As I was walking back home, I heard a loud "KABOOM" followed by seeing a flood of water flowing out from our backyard and into the street. My mother had unscrewed several of the top supports all at once. What was she thinking?

My daughter was home at the time and said, "I told grandma not to do that until you got back, but she wouldn't listen. She said it was time to tuck the liner underneath the supports."

Yes, it was time. But, it was supposed to be done one top rail at a time! So what did my mother do to get herself out of that jam? She called the pool company and told them that the liner was defective, as she was not one to take the blame for anything.

Once we sailed out to sea, I started the service by handing her sister Ann a red rose to honor her as being the sister to now take my mother's place of being the matriarch of the family.

Eight-year-old Ronny read the story of his great-great grandmother's life, she had written seven years prior which was published in a book I had created for our family.

After the Captain handed all the family and friends a long stemmed rose, he removed my mother's ashes from the white, "wise old owl" cookie jar urn to gently place her in a rose lined, linen basket. He then instructed me to kneel down to release my mother's ashes into the sea. Benjamin turned up the volume on the speakers as the song, "Mama" sung by Connie Frances, played in the background as my mother's ashes drifted out to sea. All the music and songs had been hand picked as being meaningful ones for my mother's memorial service. My husband knelt down next to share in the scattering as well as each of our four children, while family and friends tossed their roses into the sea.

Our daughter-in-law read a beautiful butterfly poem and passed around envelopes containing live butterflies to be released. We all stood out on the deck for some time calling out our good-byes.

"Let's all go do what my mom would want us to do now. Let's go eat!" I announced.

We then all returned to the cabin where a beautiful buffet with some of my mother's favorite foods awaited us.

Her sister Ann held the white, "wise old owl" cookie jar urn that had held my mother's ashes. She told me how my mother loved having lunch together with her and that she wanted to hold the urn to do so one last time.

"I remember how much Lucy loved these Subway sandwiches," she remarked.

After departing the boat, we then traveled to the cemetery by way of police escorted funeral procession. A large, beautiful heart made of red roses, from her sister Ann and Ann's daughter Mary, stood beside the wooden box our son Devin had made for his Grandma Lucy several years ago to keep her finest treasures in. My mother was so proud of her grandson's woodworking talents. She used to say that he inherited that "special gene" from me. My brother has that special gene too.

My mother's precious treasure box now contains some of her precious ashes, photos, heartfelt poems and notes, along with an inscribed "Grandma" necklace we placed inside. One from her grandson Jason and his family simply states, "Gone but not forgotten. Although we are apart, your spirit lives within us, forever in our heart."

My mother had previously said to me, she did not want to be buried. However, she had purchased a plot at the same cemetery where her parents and her late husband are buried. Most likely, she did so when she made funeral arrangements for my father, or perhaps when her parent's had died, thinking she'd one day be buried there too. I don't know. I just took advantage of that fact for one specific reason: for her to have a place on this earth for family and future generations to visit and bring flowers to place on her grave. My mother shares a headstone with my father. The simple inscription below my father's name simply reads, "Grandma Lucy, Aug 2, 1922 – Feb 7, 2015." There is a large dash in-between the dates of her life.

A Catholic Priest led the service at the cemetery speaking only of her as "Grandma Lucy." Two of her sister's great grandchildren, Doug and Brandon, each read a poem. My favorite one, "The Dash." For it was how my mother lived that dash between the dates of her birth and death that we will all remember.

Her nephew Frank stood up to tell a story about how my mother used a milkshake to lure him into the kitchen. He said it is the story he will remember most. As he told that story it seemed like it was just yesterday that I too had stood in that same kitchen waiting for my mother to make me a milkshake too in her special silver cup milkshake machine, just like the ones seen sometimes in old-fashioned soda shops.

Mary stood up to tell some stories about her Aunt Lucy that I hadn't heard before, most of which were about situations my mother would get herself in and out of.

"I remember when my Aunt Lucy insisted on buying a chair she saw in the thrift store. This wasn't just any chair. This was a chair with wheels, and said the chair would be perfect to use to scoot herself around the house in. The only problem was the thrift store wouldn't hold the chair for her until she could get someone to pick it up for her. Well, she didn't want anyone else coming along to buy that chair. What happened next was hysterical. She tied several plastic grocery bags together to make a long plastic grocery bag rope that she then used to secure the chair onto the back of her scooter with and drove it home that way herself!"

He sister nodded her head as if to say, "That's Lucy alright," confirming some of my mother's crazy antics. Her sister then stood up to say some very sincere and heartfelt words.

I stood up and placed one red rose from my brother to represent my brother's love for her and a white rose from me to represent my wish for her to rest in peace, alongside the box to be buried that contained a few of her ashes.

We then all proceeded to walk over to her parents' graves to fulfill my mother's wishes. I handed her sister the teapot that I was also filled with some of my mother's ashes. She knelt down on her parents' graves to scatter her sister's ashes on top of their headstone. I said a little prayer as her great granddaughter Katie released the big butterfly balloon from her hand into the clear blue sky. As I watched it glide it's way high up, up and away, I could hear the last goodbyes being shouted up to my mother for all the roles that she played; sister, aunt, grandmother, great grandmother, and great-great grandmother. She had impacted all of our lives in such profound, significant and purposeful ways.

Growing up in an Italian family I learned that big is better, and more is always best. I wanted to give my mother more. I had hoped that one day she would be able to travel again to all the places she loved to go, visiting family along the way. When I mentioned the idea of doing something along those lines to the mortuary they indicated that they would be able to prepare some sachet pouches, each containing a small amount of my mother's ashes to travel and be scattered by her family in specific places across the U.S. I personally took my mother to her final destination: her birthplace, which also happens to be mine in Brooklyn, New York.

And so I end and I begin a new chapter in my life.

I've learned so many lessons from my mother as a child, an adult and caregiver. The following quote says so much about what I believe my mother's wish has always been for the daughter that she raised:

"Around here
we don't look backwards for very long...
We keep moving forward,
opening up new doors and doing new things
because we're curious...
and curiosity keeps leading us down new paths."

~ Walt Disney

Ten Steps to Self-Care

1. If it feels wrong don't do it.

2. Say exactly what you mean.

3. Don't be a people pleaser.

4. Trust you instincts.

5. Never speak badly about yourself.

6. Never give up on your dreams.

7. Don't be afraid to say "No."

8. Don't be afraid to say "Yes."

9. Be kind to yourself.

10. Let go of what you can't control.

BONUS STEP: Stay away from drama and negativity as much as possible!

A CAREGIVER'S GUIDE

"Magic is believing in yourself,
if you can do that,
you can make anything happen."

~Johann Wolfgang Von Goethe

CHAPTER 6

RESTORATION

As a health coach, I am trained to recognize when to hold back and when to encourage people to forge forward. When it's personal, as it was with my mother and I, it took me quite awhile to figure out what we both needed while I cared for her. We both needed for me to stop banging my head against the wall and come to terms with the fact that when dealing with my mother it would be best if I took off all the other hats that I wear and simply be there for her, as a loving daughter. That's what your parent, needs the most from you now to. He or she simply needs you to be there as a loving son or daughter.

You'll find comfort and camaraderie by joining an online support group. Just beware you will come across a lot of complaining. And that's okay. It's healthier for caregivers to vent in order to get things off their chest than to hold in all the frustration they are feeling. Be compassionate with your words of encouragement, as they will be appreciated. Eventually someone is going to say something that you too need to hear. Keep looking for the inspirational messages your peers share with you and when you come across a joke that makes you laugh, print it out. Laughter is so healing and it truly is the best medicine. Having a good sense of humor will keep you from going crazy. There's also something to be said about giving back by helping others. You can become the beacon of hope for someone else.

"Be the change you wish to see in the world."

~ Mahatma Gandhi

As much as well meaning family and friends try to make you feel better by telling you that you are a hero for your efforts you are probably going to wish you could just smack them upside the head because there is no way that you took all this on yourself to become some sort of hero. All you really want is for someone, anyone to please help you figure out how to survive this. Let them know what you need and how they can help you.

After the initial adjustment period (I should say readjustment after readjustment period) you will be able to settle down into a more predictable (no, make that unpredictable) routine. You will feel proud of yourself for figuring out how to do things a certain way. You will know what works and what doesn't work. You will become the expert, for a little while anyway.

It's so difficult to watch your loved one declining. You may eventually reach a point where you won't know what more you can possibly do to ease the pain of your aging parent's impending helplessness. Despite the fact that their incontinence makes you gag, you'll clean it all up anyway. Keeping them safe and away from as much harm as possible is what you will do best. It's what they did for you once, too. Just keep reminding yourself of that.

What I share with you on the following pages is how I discovered what worked best for me. In my struggles, I found the strength that I needed to climb into a lifeboat to save myself from drowning. I have since helped other caregivers do the same.

The journey to self-care, in many ways, is like finding a magic lamp with a genie inside. The genie allows you to make three wishes. The only stipulation is to follow a "consistency over time" strategy in order to make each of your wishes come true.

The best place to start is to create a good foundation that you can build upon. As a caregiver with responsibilities of your own, it may seem more like a restoration process. That's okay. The most important thing to recognize is that this is the house that you will rebuild your new life upon. Build it well, to last you years.

The three wishes I'd like to suggest are:

WISH NUMBER ONE - Restore Energy

WISH NUMBER TWO - Restore Order

WISH NUMBER THREE - Restore Health

Wish Number One - Restore Energy

Energy is at the center of all life on earth. As humans, we thrive on the energy we receive from the foods we eat and our interactions with mother nature here on earth. Nothing happens without the energy we receive from the sun, the air and the water from our atmosphere.

Two ways to restore your energy are:
1. **Patch energy leaks.**
2. **Add more energy.**

1. Patch energy leaks

What are energy leaks?

Think of energy leaks as expending too much energy subjecting yourself to negativity or expending too much effort on tasks that you might be able to find a better way of doing.

In order to patch any energy leaks look for what has been dragging you down or causing you to feel drained.

For example: For me, when my mother wet the bed at night I would spend a lot of extra time and energy the following morning stripping her bed sheets as well as removing, washing and disinfecting everything that got wet before I could re-make her bed.

The way I patched that energy leak was to purchase more absorbent disposable diapers and placed disposable plastic-lined, leak proof bed pads on top of her bed sheet. In the morning all I had to do was throw the wet disposals away.

Tip: The only thing that worked for getting the urine smell washed out of the sheets and her clothing was pouring a quarter cup of white vinegar into the washing machine. White vinegar is also great for everyday cleaning for fruits and vegetables, mirrors, countertops, dishes and floors. Additionally you can add baking soda. I use it in place of toxic cleaning products all the time.

Three useful ways to patch some common energy leaks are to:

1. Stop fear in its tracks.

If your aging parent becomes riddled with fear and anxiety put a patch on it by verbally reassuring him or her that they are safe. Establish a routine for doing certain things on a regular basis that makes them feel more secure. Change the subject as soon as possible. Walk away.

2. Turn a negative into a positive.

Patch a negative behavior with positive reinforcement. If your aging parent starts complaining about something that gets them into a foul mood remind them about things that they can easily take part in or find pleasure in doing. Offer them something to do that gives them a sense of accomplishment: folding laundry, emptying the dishwasher, organizing photos, working on a puzzle, painting a paint by numbers picture, or even get them outside to tend to the garden.

3. Stand up for yourself.

When your aging parent tries to manipulate you into doing something you cannot or do not want to do, take back your power by simply saying no. If your parent is someone that you can reason with give him or her a good reason or consequence as to why you cannot do what he or she want you to do and walk away. You may also give them an alternative choice that you are more comfortable with.

For example: My mother was notorious for the tantrums she used to pull. When she wouldn't get her way, she sounded just like a two year old. I found out the hard way that the more I gave in, the more she would push me around.

Once a decision is made, stick to it. If you say you are not going to bring your father a cup of coffee before 9:00am, don't - even if you have it ready ahead of time. It's better to wait and heat it up than to confuse him by changing the routine.

Establishing set times to do certain things gives them something to look forward to and it will help you navigate through your day much more smoothly.

Creating boundaries and establishing rules also sends a clear message that you have other things to do besides wait on them all day long.

The best way to uncover your energy draining leaks is to make a list of the things that annoy you the most. Next, work out a simple solution to patch those leaks as quickly as possible.

2. Add more energy

Energy is such a precious commodity. For caregivers, needing more energy doesn't have as much to do with wanting to accomplish more things in a day, as it does with just wanting to feel better. The best way to add more energy is through the use of food. You would think that just eating better ought to do the trick, right? Not exactly.

Here are a couple of things to consider:

1. Are you eating energy-promoting foods?

You may be losing energy by not eating energy-promoting foods. When you eat foods that have very little nutritional value you end up wasting energy while your body figures out what to do with it because it is of no value to your system.

2. Are you absorbing nutrients from the food you are eating?

You may also be losing energy if you are not absorbing nutrients from the foods you are eating, due to lack of proper digestion.

Everyone has his or her own eating style. You know what foods you like and what foods you aren't crazy about. I am not going to tell you what to eat. I only want to make you aware of some ways you can eat more mindfully so that food becomes a greater source of energy for you.

If you've been eating the S̲tandard A̲merican D̲iet (S.A.D.) chances are you haven't been getting enough nutrients that you would otherwise be getting from eating vitamin rich whole foods, which are easy to assimilate and digest.

Processed foods that come in a can, jar, box or bag do not contain much, if any, energy-building nutrition. Plus, processed foods that are full of unrecognizable chemicals used to ensure a long shelf life are hard for the body to digest. Likewise, convenience foods from a fast food drive through window are loaded with excess fat and addictive sugar calories.

Do these five things to add more energy:

1. Correct any digestive issues.

Poor digestion is caused by eating too quickly, not chewing your food thoroughly enough, eating while under stress, eating too much and eating the wrong food or food combinations. Drinking warm water before meals helps to open the passageways. Drinking cold water is restricting. Water also helps lessen constipation.

2. Avoid energy-blocking constipation.

Drinking plenty of water and eating plenty of fibrous fruits and vegetables will help you move your bowels.

3. Improve nutrient absorption.

Food is absorbed through the small intestines. Even eating the right foods won't do you any good if you aren't properly absorbing their nutrients.

- Eating a little bit of good fat with your meals helps your body assimilate the nutrients found in food. Add olive oil when stir-frying vegetables and consider adding avocado and lemon to salads as lemons also help with nutrient absorption. Squeezing a little lemon juice on spinach triples iron absorption.

- Friendly bacteria found in probiotic foods also aid in breaking down food and allowing your body to use the nutrients. Eating vitamin D-rich salmon with yogurt increases calcium absorption.
- Eat raw fruits and vegetables as they contain a lot of digestive enzymes, which insure optimal nutrient absorption.

4. Eat more fiber.

Eating more fiber rich foods like beans, legumes and high quality grains aid digestion and add health-promoting nutrients into your body that is then converted into long lasting energy.

5. Exercise.

Exercising has an energy promoting affect as it lifts your mood and stimulates your organs.

- Walking is one of the best and easiest exercises you can get into the habit of doing.
- Find a warm indoor pool. It's both relaxing and easy on the joints. Take your loved one too!
- At the very least try to get into a routine where you spend a few minutes before getting out of bed to do some simple leg lifts and stretches.
- Just move any way you can and any time you can throughout the day. It all adds up.

Wish Number Two - Restore Order

Two ways to restore order in your life are:
1. **Simplified organizing**
2. **Plan your day**

When my house is a mess I feel as though my life is a mess. When you see things around you in such disarray it's easy to become unmotivated, feel sluggish, and wander aimlessly throughout your day. If you are finding that each day starts and ends the same way as the previous one without accomplishing much of anything, it's time to get organized.

I found out the hard way that there's a right way and a wrong way to go about getting organized. It's doubly difficult when you have an aging parent living in your house, occupying extra space with a walker, commode and other medically necessary devices.

I can't tell you how many times I reorganized the furniture in my mother's room and cleared clutter from her closets and drawers. She was pretty good about letting me go through her stuff, but it's important to keep in mind that as people age they have a very hard time adapting to change. Older people also may have a hard time making decisions. Staying as clutter-free as possible will cut down on many of these issues.

1. Simplified organizing

Five simple ways to get and stay organized:

1. Use paper goods.

If you allow your aging parent to eat or drink in their bed-room, simplify your work by providing them with paper goods. I don't like eating off paper plates or drinking from a paper cup, but having a pile of dishes in the sink at the end of the day is worse.

Tip: Two tips I learned while working in a professional kitchen to cut down being stuck with a sink full of pots and pans are
1. Wash, dry and put away pots and pans as you use them.
2. The only pots and pans that require you using soap are ones with any grease or sticky residue on them, since soap cuts through the grease. You can simply rinse the others unless you have someone in the house eating out of them.

---

2. Make things easy to find.

I know that it works for many caregivers to label drawers, but it never worked for my mother. She was notorious at misplacing things because she never put things back where they belonged. In fact, she'd often put things in the strangest places. My solution was to just buy duplicates of the things she used most often.

On the other hand, I love having separation organizers in drawers for same type items, especially kitchen and desk drawers.

3. Rotate seasonal clothes.

Most people tend to wear the same five or six outfits per season over and over again. That's all anyone really needs, ten tops. If you organize the clothes in your closet seasonally you will always look appropriately dressed. Start with placing your five to ten spring clothes together, followed by your summer outfits, then your fall and winter ones. As the seasons change move those clothes to the other side of your closet.

4. Use a filing system.

It's a good idea to keep your parent's medical information, contact phone numbers, and financial records in a well-organized place that is easily accessible. Seniors tend to be hoarders to a certain degree. I remember how my Aunt Barbara kept old checks and receipts for things she purchased, dating to way back when. If they insist on keeping old papers in a box, put them in a separate room, a dedicated clutter-saver closet. Out of sight, out of mind.

5. Maintain clutter-free surroundings.

- Keep your parent's bedroom as clutter-free as possible and keep knick-knacks throughout your house at a minimum.
- Throw rugs are not only tripping hazards they can make a room look cluttered.
- Whenever possible, place photos of loved ones on a wall, instead of arranging them on tabletop furniture. In my opinion, the only practical things to place on tabletop furniture are lamps and plants.

- Plants help oxygenate and improve the air quality in your home.

The rule in our house is that everything we bring into the house has to have a designated place. If we can't find a practical place for it, it doesn't belong in our house. It's a simple rule to follow.

---

2. Plan your day

Seven easy planning techniques:

1. Make a to-do list.

Making a to-do list of things you would like to accomplish is a tool you can use to either guide you through your day or remind you of things you would like to get done. Follow these three simple steps to make your to-do list work for you.

2. Prioritize your to-do list.

When there are items on your to-do list that are more important to get done before other items, list those items first.

3. Keep your to-do list short.

Realize that there are only so many things that can realistically be accomplished within a certain time frame. What works best for me is to have a running list of extra things, aside from daily chores, that I would like to accomplish on a separate sheet of paper. I then choose three to five extra things from that larger list to put on my daily to-do list.

4. Be flexible, but don't procrastinate.

If there are things on your list that never seem to get done, take them off the list for now. You can always add them back on later.

5. Create a weekly schedule.

There are certain days throughout the week when I do certain things at certain times on an ongoing basis. Writing these things down in a day planner or other time management system will allow you to see what you spend your time doing. Seeing your daily life on paper, allows you to see if you are being fair enough to yourself. If your life doesn't look balanced make adjustments from there.

6. Leave space for spontaneity.

Don't fill in every waking moment. After all, you are not a machine. If there is a scheduled day that you might have available to attend a class or activity you enjoy, don't add washing and setting your mother's hair on that same day. Leave extra time to spontaneously take your mother out to lunch.

7. Use a pencil.

Expect to have things come from time to time. Instead of ending up with a messy looking calendar with a bunch of scratch-out items it's best to pencil in appointments and activities that can be easily erased.

Scheduling your day this way guides you through your week more efficiently.

A GIFT FOR YOU

I'd like to support you on your journey back to health and well-being by sending you a FREE little magic lamp charm as my special gift of encouragement to you.

To receive your little magic lamp in silver or bronze please send a self-addressed-stamped envelope (*return envelope requires 2 stamps*) to my office at:

Elaine Lombardi
24001 Calle De La Magdalena, Suite 8043
Laguna Hills, CA 92653

Indicate your preference of silver or bronze. If you would also like my mother's famous Italian Cream Puffs recipe and receive my newsletter please include your email address.

Wish Number Three - Restore Health

Wish number three is all about restoring your health by building a self-care routine. One of the most important things to remember is that when things are not easy to do we don't want to do them. That will not be the case here.

The things I introduce you to in the following chapter are easy. Trust me, you are going to love getting into the kind of self-care routine that will rejuvenate you in more ways than one. You will enjoy pampering yourself this way.

Before we delve into building your self-care routine, let me share a secret with you.

The secret to restoring your health

The best way to restore your health is to make the process of doing so your own. You won't be happy establishing a self-care routine you will want to stick with if you aren't doing things that you like and want to do. So, here's some advice for you:

Start with passion.

*"Find something you are passionate about
and keep tremendously interested in it."*

~ Julia Child

Passion comes from you being authentic and feeling free to do what comes naturally to you. When what you do is in alignment with who you are, you feel more alive from doing it. The more passionate you are about something, the more momentum you'll generate to stay on a your purposeful path.

Discovering and claiming something you love to do, has an amazing affect on your entire life. Most of us have a natural aptitude or knack for of doing something that makes us feel comfortable and happy or occupies our thoughts with a yearning to get back to doing.

Sometimes we don't recognize a talent until someone else points it out to us. Having someone else see your talent, in a way gives you permission to fully embrace it. Identifying things you love that you're good at is a great way to awaken your passions.

You don't necessarily need to be good at something for it to qualify as a passion. When it comes to your passions, the only thing that matters is that you enjoy what you are passionate about.

Three Ways to awaken your passion

1. Do more of what you love.

If you love planning parties, help others by suggesting ways you can help them plan a party they may be having.

2. Do what makes you feel like a kid again.

Find a comfortable way to do so in an adult way.

3. Pay attention to your desires.

Recognize what you long to have more time for and schedule time for it.

Having more passion in your life is really just about turning adversity into adventure and challenges into opportunities.

Keep in mind, every action, or inaction, is a choice that you make everyday.

Make a conscious decision to change any tendency you may have towards negative thoughts by breaking the patterns that have held you back from achieving a full and passionate life.

"The real voyage of discovery consists not in seeking new landscapes but in having new eyes."

~Marcel Proust

CHAPTER 7

YOUR LIFEBOAT

The tips I share with you in this section of the book are all part of The H.E.A.L. Approach Program I developed to help caregivers build a self-care routine that will work for them. H.E.A.L. stands for <u>H</u>ealthy <u>E</u>ating <u>A</u>ctive <u>L</u>ife.

I use these same strategies in my own self-care routine and have since helped many caregivers build their own. There's no one-size-fits-all. Building a self-care routine that will fit comfortably into your own life is an ongoing process of setting goals for the improvements you'd like to make.

Although your self-care routine will be uniquely your own, I want you to know that you are not alone in the process of creating it. We're all in this together. I've created a special online community blog that I'd like to personally invite you to participate in.

Subscribe to the newsletter, read the blog, post comments and participate in the conversations by submitting your own stories. Go check it out today! www.healthcoachforcaregivers.com.

Please also feel free to personally contact me for further assistance or questions you may have. I'd love hearing from you. Email me or visit my website where I share healthy recipes and other beneficial tips.

Email: Elaine@ElaineLombardi.com
Website: www.ElaineLombardi.com

"In order to love who you are,
you can't hate the experiences
that shaped you."

~ Andrea Dykstra

Building Your Self Care Routine

The airlines got it right when they instruct you to put your own oxygen mask on first. When we are well taken care of we automatically feel so much better about taking care of others. One of the first rewards you're likely to notice is that you feel like you're getting your life back.

Building your self-care routine isn't going to be about doing boring things that you'd rather not be doing. Remember the secret to restoring your health is to make the process of doing so your own, make it something you like and can look forward to doing. Think of it as your time.

Would you like to see an example of my daily routine?

I'd be happy to send it to you along with a printable fill in the blanks worksheet that you can use to easily create your own daily routine. Simply send an email to Elaine@ElaineLombardi.com. Please put DAILY ROUTINE in the subject line of your email request.

Tip: You may want to also consider helping your loved ones establish a routine as well. Doing so will give them a sense of independence and security through familiarity.

Within the next few pages I will teach you what I believe is the easiest, most effective way to restore your health (and your loved one's) in the least amount of time possible. Just because the techniques I share with you don't take a lot of time to implement, doesn't mean they don't have to be ongoing. That's the key. Consistency over time is where all the magic takes place.

It's not necessary to adopt everything all at once. It's the accumulation of the small things that you do that have the biggest impact on your health. When you follow a regular ongoing routine, real change is possible. A slow and steady approach allows enough time for you to adapt and evolve. Once you reach and adapt to a certain level of proficiency, you may wish to progress and evolve to a higher level of achievement and proficiency.

Your Self-Care Tool Kit

1. **Revitalize Your Nutrition** - Food Changes everything
2. **Jumpstart Your Lymphatic System** – Rebounding
3. **Energize Your Whole Body** - Earthing
4. **Stimulate Detoxification** - Body Brushing and Detox Baths
5. **Restorative Rest** - Nighttime Routine
6. **Managing Stress** - Checklist

1. Revitalize Your Nutrition

I am not an advocate of strict diets and I don't believe in any one dietary theory over another. The whole concept of being well nourished with all systems working as efficiently as possible is really the definition of health. It's also the definition of preventing disease.

Food changes everything

"Every time you eat or drink
you are either
feeding disease or fighting it."

~Anonymous

Diets don't usually address such things as seasonal changes that can affect our eating choices and desires. It's not uncommon to find yourself craving certain things at certain times of year, or during certain holidays or special occasions. We attach a lot of meanings and feelings to food. It can even seem as though the world revolves around food!

Of all the diet programs out there, I believe that the following ten power-packed common sense practices, form the foundation for a well-balanced, nutritional way of eating.

Note: I have provided a recipe section in the back of the book that contains some of my favorite quick and easy recipes from my personal collection.

Ten steps to revitalize your nutrition:

1. **Start each day by drinking a warm glass of lemon water.**
   Lemon is a natural energizer that hydrates and oxygenates your body. Drinking lemon water will boost your immune system.

2. **Eat a small portion of protein with every meal.**
   Proteins are the building blocks for a large part of the functional and structural components of our body. It doesn't matter whether you get most of your protein from animals or plants. I believe a combination of both sources is important.

3. **Eat carbohydrates daily.**
   Many people who have become accustomed to eating low carb diets are missing the most efficient source of energy: carbohydrates. Carbohydrates are present in all plants, including fruits, vegetables, seeds, rice, beans and grains. Carbohydrates are what help us digest our food more efficiently.

4. **Eat healthy fats with vegetables**
   Think of fat as brain food. Good choices of healthy fat include: avocados, grass fed butter, coconut oil, olive oil, almond butter, cashews, and ground flax seeds or flax seed oil. A great way to add fat to your diet is to add a healthy fat to vegetables. Adding a healthy fat to vegetables helps your body more easily absorb the valuable nutrients found in them.

5. **Eat a small amount of probiotic food with your meals.**
   Probiotic foods repopulate friendly bacteria into your gut with the right kind of acids in your stomach and enzymes in your

intestines. Fermented foods such as pickles, kim chi (made from cultured vegetables), yogurt and kefir (made from cultured dairy milks), and miso (made from fermented soybeans) are good choices.

6. **Drink nutrient rich green juices and nutritionally dense protein smoothies.**

Both are great. What's the difference? Juice without the pulp will be absorbed into the blood system more quickly. Using a juicer that separates the pulp will do that. Using blender to puree fruits and vegetables into a smoothie leaves the fiber intact. Just remember that it will take longer to digest a smoothie due to the fiber in it. You can also add a variety of other ingredients into a smoothie to make it a complete and nourishing meal. For better nutritional absorption, add a healthy fat such as an avocado. Also consider adding Super foods such Maca powder, Spirulina and Chlorella, as well as high protein hemp seeds. These Super foods can all be purchased at most local health food stores.

Tip: When a very sick person needs a quick nutritional boost use a juicer for faster absorption of nutrients. Using a blender prolongs the digestive process.

---

7. **Eat Sprouts.**

Another great way to eat more nutritionally dense foods is to use sprouts. Add sprouts to salads and sandwiches and green smoothies. Sprouts are rich in essential vitamins, minerals, protein, fiber and omega-3 fatty acids. Sprouts are also an excellent source of enzymes, which are lost in cooked foods.

8. Make homemade bone broth.

One of the most nutritious foods you can make from leftover meat bones is bone broth. Don't throw the chicken, turkey carcass or the beef bones from a roast away.

The body easily absorbs mineral rich nutrients from home-made bone broth. Bone broth contains calcium, magnesium, phosphorus and other trace minerals. It does wonders for arthritis sufferers as it contains glucosamine and chondroitin, which helps to alleviate joint pain. Drink it as a tonic or add some stock vegetables for a hearty soup.

9. Soak and sprout certain foods before consuming them.

Soaking seeds before roasting them and beans and rice before cooking them removes enzyme inhibitors. Soaking these foods sprouts or enlivens them, which adds nutritional value. Eating naturally sprouted sourdough breads are much more nutritious than conventional yeast rising breads.

10. Eat more seasonally grown fruits and vegetables.

When you buy produce that is in season you will get more bang for you buck. Seasonal produce is less expensive and contains more nutrients from being picked closer to its peak of ripeness, especially locally grown produce that doesn't have far to travel.

It's easy to incorporate more vegetables into the foods you eat when you know how to do it. Look through the recipe section at the end of this book for recipes that add vegetables to pasta sauce, soups, spreads, sandwich fixings and omelets.

2. Jumpstart your Lymphatic System

Toxins get inside our body by way of pollutants present in the air we breathe and the water we drink. There are also toxic chemicals in the foods we eat and the lotions that we put on our bodies.

Our lymphatic system is designed to carry these toxins out of the body. Other systems also detoxify and work to cleanse the body.

Rebounding
(mini trampoline)

What is a rebounding?

Rebounding is jumping up and down on a rebounder, otherwise known as a mini trampoline. It's a great way to stimulate the flow of removing toxins is by doing rebounding.

Just ten minutes of rebounding is as effective as 30 minutes of jogging. A great way to stimulate the flow of removing toxins is by doing rebounding.

Seven health benefits of rebounding are:
1. Increased muscular strength.
2. Improved balance and coordination.
3. Reduction in stress.
4. Weight loss.
5. Improved blood flow, circulation and internal organ stimulation.
6. Elimination of toxins through the lymphatic system.
7. More energy with an overall sense of wellbeing.

Even just 2 minutes of rebounding a day works wonders. You do not need to jump high or even long to benefit from rebounding.

Exercise helps to simulate your body. The best way to use a rebounder to jumpstart your lymphatic system, to remove toxins, is to start with a few jumping jacks. Your arms act like a pump by moving them up and down as you would while doing jumping jacks on the ground.

You will get a great workout while rebounding. Be creative but be careful. For a safer and secure rebounding experience purchase a mini-trampoline or professional rebounder that has a stabilizing bar attached to it.

Don't have a rebounder? No problem. Don't let it keep you from reaping the benefits. You will still get a good workout simply by moving your heels up and down on the floor as you pump your arms. If you have a stability ball, bouncing your butt up and down on it will get your lymphatic system stimulated too. Keep this in mind: *"Where there's a will, there's a way."* So JUMP!

WARNING: Elderly people can lose their balance easily. Play it safe. Don't allow them to use a rebounder unattended or attempt to move their feet without holding onto something steady. They will still benefit if all they can safely do is move their arms up and down like a pump.

A word about EFT. EFT (Emotional Freedom Technique) "tapping" is a wonderful way to help relieve emotional blocks within the body. This is very easy to learn. Use this technique on yourself or your loved one. For further information regarding the EFT technique visit the website www.emofree.com.

Learning EFT accupressure, Reiki and reflexology techniques will help you and your loved one balance energy flow in the body.

3. Energize Your Whole Body

Do you realize that the earth is a giant battery filled with electric energy and that the skin is a natural conductor of electricity? When we are "grounded" or connected to the earth, free electrons from the earth transfer into our bodies.

Earthing

Researchers Dr. Christy Westen and Dr. James Oschman have proven that these electrons decrease inflammation, reduce pain, promote healthy sleep and thin the blood, which helps reduce heart disease.

We were much more directly connected to the earth when we spent more time walking and working outside. Now we spend most of our time indoors in high-rise buildings, wearing rubber-soled (electrically insulated) or plastic shoes. Wood, asphalt and vinyl are not conductive surfaces and will not work well for Earthing.

Get outdoors more often to reap the benefits that Earthing will bring. You can get "earthed" today by simply going outside and walking barefoot on the ground or by standing or lying on the grass. It only takes a few minutes to become revitalized from the ground up!

Just as the sun gives us warmth and vitamin D, the earth gives us food, water and a surface to walk on. Think of it as vitamin G for Good health by way of Grounding.

Tip: Ask your parent to join you too!

4. Stimulate Detoxification

Toxins in the body may cause symptoms such as fatigue, depression, body aches, insomnia and the inability to concentrate. Your body is designed to naturally cleanse itself. You can help it along by being mindful of pollutants in the air you breathe and the water you drink, as well as any chemicals in products you put on your body that gets transferred through your skin.

Your skin is the largest cleansing and detoxifying organ of the body.

Two methods to remove toxins through your skin:
1. Body Brushing.
2. Detox Baths.

Your skin needs to breathe. Dirt, soap residue and body lotions that you put on your skin can clog your pours. This type of cleansing is best accomplished through body brushing.

1. Body Brushing

Body brushing is a simple technique that stimulates blood and lymphatic flow, improves circulation, massages deep internal organs, exfoliates the skin and encourages new cell growth. Body brushing brings nutrients and oxygen to the outer layers of skin.

To get started, buy a natural bristle brush. Body brushing is done with a dry brush on dry skin.

The instructions for body brushing are simple.

Nine Key Points:

1. Start at your feet brushing your skin using long sweeping strokes.
2. Brush up towards your heart to encourage a return of blood and encourage lymphatic flow.
3. The only exception is the back. Start at the back of your neck brushing down to the lower back.
4. Brushing too hard on your thighs may break tiny blood vessels and create broken veins or capillaries.
5. Be gentle on your breasts and face and don't forget to brush your ears.
6. Brush your abdomen in a circular clock-wise motion.
7. Brush your arms with an upward motion, moving towards your heart.
8. Apply a natural moisturizer or coconut oil afterwards to nourish your skin.
9. Drink plenty of water to help flush out toxins.

The whole process takes no more than two to five minutes. Do it first thing in the morning when the increased blood flow will help to wake you up. Or do it before you take a shower.

Tip: If you have sensitive skin, wet a soft washcloth and wet stroke your skin in the bath or shower with a natural soap or soap free cleanser. The water will help reduce the friction caused by body brushing. Use this technique on it on your parent too!

2. Detox Baths

A detox bath will assist your body in eliminating toxins as well as absorbing the minerals and nutrients that are in the water.

To prepare a detox bath you will need:
Epsom salts
Baking soda
Ginger (optional)
Lavender or other aromatherapy essential oils (optional)

Directions:

1. Add 2 cups of Epsom salts to warm bath water.
Soaking in Epsom salts helps replenish the body's magnesium level, flushes toxins and helps form proteins in brain tissue and joints.

2. Add 1 cup of baking soda.
Baking soda is known for its cleansing ability and anti-fungal properties. It also leaves skin very soft.

3. Add 1 Tablespoon of ground ginger or fresh ginger tea.
Although this step is optional ginger can increase your heat levels, helping to sweat out toxins.

4. Add 10 drops of Lavender or other essential oils.
Again optional, but many people love the fragrance of such oils. Essential oils also have therapeutic properties to take advantage of.

5. After your bath drink plenty of water.

Any time your body detoxes you need to flush out toxins internally by drinking water. If you skip this step, you will likely feel sick afterwards.

It is also a good idea to rub down your body with a Loofah sponge to help stimulate lymph flow to aid with the release of toxins.

Speaking of detoxification, **Oil pulling** is an ancient Ayurvedic therapy believed to promote oral health and detoxification. The instructions are simple. You simply swish a couple teaspoons of either coconut, sesame, olive oil in your mouth for 10 - 20 minutes. Then spit it out, followed by rinsing your mouth out with water. The oil mixes with your saliva, turning it into a thin, white liquid. Lipids in the oil pull out toxins from the saliva as an efficient detoxifier. As the oil is swished around in the mouth, it continues to absorb toxins and usually ends up turning thick, viscous, and white. Once the oil has reached this consistency (typically after ten minutes), it is spit out before the toxins are reabsorbed.

"On particularly rough days,
when I'm sure I can't possibly endure,
I like to remind myself
that my track record for getting through
so far is 100%
and that's pretty good."

~ Anonymous

*"Your future depends on
your dreams,
So go to sleep."*

~ Mesut Barazany

5. Restorative Rest

Sleep is an essential component for both physical and emotional health. Sleep also fosters creativity, which can improve mood and help cultivate a positive attitude. Getting enough sleep at night plays an important role in life itself.

During sleep, your body and psyche are both regaining their strength for the coming day. Meanwhile, your long-term memories are reinforced.

How much sleep you need depends upon where you are in life. Young people often need more sleep, while older people may need less. On average it's a good idea to shoot for eight hours of sleep a night. Regular and consistent periods of wakefulness and sleep are key ingredients to fostering a healthy body and a clear mind. It is during sleep that your body renews itself.

Nighttime Routine

Establishing a calming evening routine can help. Start early by dimming the lights and turning down the noise produced by the TV. Reading a book in bed has a hypnotic sleepy-time affect on many people. Spend a few minutes journaling to get things off your chest. Yoga, meditation and deep breathing can improve the quality of your sleep by inducing full body relaxation and a deep meditative state of consciousness. Give yourself the gift of peaceful slumber and you will likely find yourself feeling alert, refreshed, and ready for life's challenges. You may also find yourself feeling more centered, thoughtful, and aware throughout the day so you can live up to your full potential and have energy for caregiving.

Managing Stress Checklist

☐ **Smile.**

Finding something to smile about will instantly lift your mood. Come on. Go ahead and turn that frown upside down. Now let out a little laugh. Fake it if you have to. Remember to keep in mind that laughter is the best medicine.

☐ **Get some fresh air.**

Go outside everyday. Even if it's only for a few minutes getting a breath of fresh air can be invigorating. If it's not possible to walk outside, open a window or at least look out one. The change in scenery will do you good.

☐ **Fit in some exercise.**

Movement is a natural stress reliever. Get in the habit of walking, if nothing else. You can go to a yoga or tai chi class or find these type and many other exercise videos to play on your television. You can also dance your way around the house as you vacuum. Put some music on and shake your booty.

☐ **Do something for yourself.**

It's crucial that you find time for yourself to pursue a hobby or connect with friends. Neglecting your own physical and emotional health leaves you vulnerable to disease and exhaustion.

☐ **Eat a well balanced diet.**

You can't function properly if your body isn't properly nourished.

☐ **Read, meditate and pray.**

Do something that brings you spiritual comfort and relief. Do it every day without fail.

☐ **Learn to relax.**

Stress causes tension in your muscles. Doing thins like stretching or taking a hot shower has a relaxing affect on your system.

☐ **Breathe.**

To oxygenate your body and reduce stress immediately, use Dr. Andrew Weil's 4-7-8 Relaxing Breathing technique. According to Dr. Weil, this type of breathing is a "natural tranquilizer for the nervous system."

Here's what you do:

1. Place the tip of your tongue so it's touching the roof of your mouth, slightly up against the back of your top teeth.
2. Exhale completely, making a whooshing sound.
3. Close your mouth and inhale through your nose for 4 counts.
4. Hold your breath for 7 counts.
5. Exhale through your mouth for 8 counts.

Repeat the cycle 4 times.

"CHANGE Every one of us alone has the power
to direct the course of our lives
by choosing what actions
we will or won't take.
While sometimes it's easier
to believe you don't have a choice,
the reality is that
you always have a choice to
behave and think differently."

~Francine Wardi

CHAPTER 8

SILVER LININGS

A gift is something you give someone. That someone can be you. You can be your own giver and receiver. When caregivers become overly involved in caring for their aging parent's needs they tend to forget how to become the receiver. You may even resign yourself to believe that your parent has used up all the gifts they have to give you. I beg to differ with you on that.

There's a very special bond that always exists between a parent and a child, no matter how old you both become. Often referred to as "unconditional love" there will always be a give and take relationship between the two of you through the bond you share. No one and nothing can or will ever be able to take that away from you. Not even the terrible disease of Alzheimer's. The gift is based on "silent whispers."

What are silent whispers?

Silent whispers are all the feelings behind the words that are written in our hearts.

Sometimes, in times of trouble or distance we forget that the bond is there. But, it's important to remember, no matter how mean and ornery a parent becomes in their lifetime, or how angry or hurt a child becomes throughout their life, this special silent whispers bond is indestructible.

You can rekindle your bond with your parent instantly at any-time. It only takes a simple touch of your hand, for the messages of the heart to travel through to one another, once again.

When you think about it, most elderly people don't get a chance to have very much tender loving touch time anymore. In many instances, by the time they need care their spouse is deceased and their grandchildren are grown along with all those tender loving bear hugs. About the only touching they receive is when they are changed, given a quick sponge bath or receiving some help to get dressed. After awhile we tend to do all these things rather mechanically just to get them done as quickly as possible.

On the days that I washed my mother's hair I decided to spend a little extra time giving her a relaxing scalp massage. By doing so, I discovered just how relaxing it became for me too. I also found that taking time to put lotion on her skin and polish her fingernails went a long way to making her feel good, which lifted her mood tremendously. When she felt good, I felt good about making her feel good. It's true what they say, "what goes around, comes around." It's contagious that way.

Homegrown Happiness

Happiness is contagious. When someone walks into a room *all smiles* you may have noticed that your curiosity kicks in with a yearning to know why they are so happy. They seem to sparkle and shine as though they are covered in fairy dust. You may even find that the affect they have on you starts to turn your frown upside down into a smile too. When I see someone so happy like that, I instinctively tend to be drawn closer to that person. I want a piece of what they have. Don't you?

Why is it that some people seem so happy all the time? It seems like these people always have something nice to say. I think it's because they are filled with gratitude without a negative bone in their body.

They appear to have such a positive attitude about everything. But maybe they have had trials and tribulations in their life too. For some, maybe even far more tragic than any of the ones you have had.

Do you ever wonder what church they might go to for giving them such a strong sense of faith? Perhaps, they do go to church, but maybe not. Spirituality plays a big role in a person's faith, no matter what they believe in and how they live their life. Whether faith has been instilled in you since birth or you stumble upon it, it's all very personal. Spend time thinking about it to see what resonates with you.

I think faith has a lot to do with getting glimpses into your purpose or the meaning of your life. In that way, faith is a guiding force. At times we may follow someone else's lead. There's certainly nothing wrong with adopting someone else's beliefs as our own.

Happiness is the same. Have you ever heard the expression, "Happiness is an inside job?" Obviously, when someone is happy it's going to show on the outside in some way. Stir up a dose of happiness, even if only momentarily for yourself. You never know who else might benefit from it too, by getting a glimpse of yours.

I recently learned something that put the whole happiness thing into perspective for me.

When happiness is an <u>inside</u> job it becomes our guide. It's something that is present right here and now, to guide us along our path. It brings out the best in us.
BUT –
When we make happiness an <u>outside</u> job it becomes a destination, a "maybe" kind of thing that is always in the distance and never really present.

In this regard, you can either <u>choose or chase happiness</u>.

The same holds true for joy. The expression, "You bring out the joy in me," is indicative of the fact that we already own the feeling of joy. Joy flows from the same source as happiness, love and peace. It flows from your heart.

Right now, going through what you may be going through, it's okay to need a little extra guidance in order to bring joy closer to the surface.

Ten Ways to Choose Joy

See what resonates with you to bring the joy back into your life and your home:

1. **Walk** to your local park to spend time watching children, pets and positive people enjoying the outdoors.
2. **Read** a children's book.
3. **Find a Laughter Yoga class.** Stay for the whole class because the end is usually the best! Go as often as you can.
4. **Make a gratitude list.** Don't hide behind what once was. Remember the joyful moments of it all. That's where gratitude comes from anyway.
5. **Teach someone** to do something you enjoy doing. You just may find a partner in crime that way.
6. **Do a random act of kindness.** It can be as simple as pulling out a grocery cart for someone who walked in the store behind you.
7. **Strike up a conversation** with someone who's standing or sitting next to you. Ask them "What's new and good in your life?" You'll be amazed how that simple question can make someone's day!
8. **Decorate your home** for all the different seasons, even if it feels silly. It doesn't have to be a holiday to spread that kind of cheer.
9. **Spend quality time** with your family. A great activity that everyone can get involved in is to color or play go fish.
10. **Bring an animal into your home**, even if only for a visit. Animals help people exercise their desire to show affection.

Bonus Tip: Hug! Hug as often as you can.

"We do not heal the past by dwelling there.
We heal the past by living in the present."

~ Marianne Williamson

CHAPTER 9

WASHED ASHORE

Your food choices each day affect your health and how you feel today, tomorrow, and in the future.

Good nutrition is an important part of leading a healthy lifestyle. The link between good nutrition and healthy weight, reduced chronic disease risk, and overall health is too important to ignore. By taking steps to eat healthy, you'll be on your way to getting the nutrients your body needs to stay healthy, active, and strong.

I've put together a collection of some of my most favorite healthy recipes that are quick and so easy to make, mostly from scratch. There's also a bunch of tips mixed in too! Visit my website at www.elainelombardi.com for a whole lot more.

I'll let you in on a little secret... I hardly ever measure the ingredients I use. So, don't sweat the small stuff, okay? If you don't happen to have a certain ingredient on hand, do what I do - improvise. The only measuring I do - is when I bake. You just can't break the rules when it comes to baking!

Ready to put on your chef's hat and have some fun learning some new healthy recipes?

*"You don't have to cook
fancy or complicated masterpieces –
just good food
from fresh ingredients."*

~ Julia Child

My Favorite Healthy Recipes and Tips

"*I always think if you have to cook once,
it should feed you twice.
If you're going to make a big chicken
and vegetable soup for lunch on Monday,
you stick it in the refrigerator
and it's also for Wednesday's dinner.*"

~ Curtis Stone

Bone Broth and Soups

One of the most nutritious things you can make from leftover beef bones or the carcass of chicken, or turkey bones is bone broth. Don't throw the bones away!

Five Benefits of Bone Broth:

1. **Good for your gut.**
   The gelatin in bone broth protects and heals the mucosal lining of the digestive tract and helps aid in the digestion of nutrients.

2. **Fights infections.**
   During a respiratory infection eating chicken soup helps reduce the number of white blood cells, which are the cells that cause flu and cold symptoms.

3. **Reduces joint pain and inflammation.**
   The glucosamine in bone broth can actually stimulate the growth of new collagen, repair damaged joints and reduce pain and inflammation.

4. **Helps with bone formation, growth and repair.**
   The calcium, magnesium and phosphorus in bone broth helps bones to grow and repair.

5. **Promotes sleep and calms the mind.**
   The amino acid glycine found in bone broth is calming.

Drink homemade bone broth as a tonic or add some stock vegetables to it for a hearty beef stew or chicken soup.

While the thought of making your own bone broth may seem intimidating at first, it's actually quite easy. All you need is a stockpot or crockpot full of water and the bones you are going to use. Add any extra nutrition and flavorings to the following recipe.

Simple Bone Broth Recipe

Ingredients: (no need to measure)

Chicken or Turkey Bones

2 Tbsp. apple cider vinegar

Optional. However, the acidity helps to draw out
a lot more nutrients from the bones.

1 large onion - cut in quarter's skin and all.

The skin contains a lot of nutrients.

2 carrots - do not peel or chop ends off.

There are a lot of nutrients found in the skin and root ends.

3 celery stalks

Or just chop off and toss in about 3 inches of the celery root end.

1 bunch of parsley.

Parsley is one of the most nutritious greens available.

Directions:

1. Place the chicken or turkey bones, carcass and all in a large stockpot or crockpot.
2. Fill with water.
3. Add other ingredients.

4. Bring all to boil.

5. Cover and simmer for several hours.

   If using a crockpot leave on low overnight.

Let cool.

6. Strain and discard everything but the clear broth.

7. Place in glass jars.

8. Place in refrigerator.

9. Skim off any excess fat that has risen to the surface.

Use within 3-4 days. Can be frozen up to 6 months.

Note: Use the same recipe for beef bone broth too!

Turn it into a Hearty Soup

To make a hearty chicken or turkey soup sauté one chopped onion in some olive oil. Add in some cut up vegetables. I like to use celery and carrots. Sometimes I add other vegetables that I have in the house like peas, cut up green beans, zucchini and even tomatoes.

For a really hearty soup add orzo pasta and barley or you can just use any kind of pasta you have. Rice is also good. No need to measure. Just keep in mind that when you add pasta it will expand. If you don't think you have enough broth, just add more water. If you want to add beans, I suggest you soak them and cook the beans separately ahead of time. You can also precook your pasta. Doing so will give you a clearer looking broth as the pasta leaves behind some starchy cloudiness.

You can add just about anything you like as a seasoning, even salsa! Yep, when I want a hint of a tomato base, tangy tortilla type soup I add in some salsa. Boil everything until it's tender then at the last minute put in your left over cooked chicken or turkey chunks. Top with Parmesan cheese. Garnish with fresh parsley (use cilantro in place of parsley for tortilla soup). Add croutons or serve with your favorite crackers. For tortilla soup add tortilla strips.

Secrets of Making Great Tasting Soups

The Basics.

Start by sautéing some diced onions in a little butter to deepen the flavor of any soup you are making.

It's best to use the same pot for everything. There's a lot of flavor that gets captured in the pot that you'll want to scrap away at before you pour your soup into another container. Leeks especially, add a tremendous amount of flavor to soups.

When adding garlic, you still want to sauté it in a pan, but use a separate pan and add the garlic to your soup during the last 10 minutes as garlic tends to get bitter the longer it cooks.

Order of adding ingredients.

When adding ingredients, always try to add longer cooking ingredients before ones that don't take as long to cook. For instance, add carrots before quicker cooking zucchini.

Beans.

When adding beans, always soak first and then cook them separately ahead of time, then add them into your soup towards the end.

Pasta, Rice and Starches.

Depending on how starchy a grain or vegetable is, such as pasta or potatoes, before adding it decide how clear and how thick you want your finished soup to be.

To make a thicker soup cook them in as you cook the soup. For thinner soups cook them separately and rinse in cold water before adding them to the soup towards the end.

Keep in mind that pasta, rice and barley will expand by soaking up a lot of liquid as it cooks, so you may need to add extra water.

Color.

Some vegetables will leach a lot of color into the broth, such as beets or greens. Remember we eat with our eyes, so when using some colorful vegetables be mindful of the outcome and use them creatively.

Adding meat.

You can use the meat from the discarded bones but all the nutrients have been sucked out of them and into the broth. When adding additional meat it's best to judge how long it should cook and then add it to the soup at that time. Remember that chicken breast cooks rather quickly. If overcook them they texture will be woody.

Consistency.

Soup can be any consistency you want. To make soup thinner, add water. To make soup thicker, puree some of the starchy vegetables in a blender, or stir in arrowroot powder as a thickener.

Creamy soups .

When making creamed soup, always use fresh dairy to prevent curdling.

Pureed soups.

You can turn any soup into a pureed or even semi-pureed more chunky soup by simply blending the ingredients together after cooking the soup.

Finishing Touches.

Add freshness to your soups by adding herbs such as parsley as a garnish last. Always use fresh herbs whenever possible. Other nice additions that add texture and contrasting flavors are a dollop of plain Greek yogurt, which goes especially well in sweet potato and squash soups, croutons or crackers!

My Favorite Quick Change Soup Tip: Short on time, or wish to add some zip to your soup? Add salsa! Works great, especially when wanting to make a chicken tortilla soup.

Quick Tomato Soup

Here's all you do:

1. Open up a small can of tomato sauce.
2. Add water to make it the consistency you want.
3. Heat thoroughly through in a pot on the stove.
4. Add salsa to taste.
5. Add a dollop of plain great yogurt

Adding More Fruits and Veggies

Eating from a rainbow of different colored fruits and vegetables ensures that you receive a variety of nutrients that benefit your body.

Red
Improves heart and blood health as well as support joints.

Orange
Prevents cancer and promotes collagen growth.

Yellow
Helps the heart, vision, digestion and immune system.

Green
Detoxifies you immune system to fight free radicals.

Blue/Purple
Contains powerful anti-oxidants.

White
Activates our natural killer cells for a reduced cancer risk.

Dirty Dozen

Always buy organic

1. Apples
2. Peaches
3. Nectarines
4. Strawberries
5. Grapes
6. Celery
7. Spinach
8. Sweet Bell Peppers
9. Cucumbers
10. Cherry Tomatoes
11. Snap Peas
12. Potatoes
+ Hot Peppers,
Kale, Collard Greens

Clean Fifteen

1. Avocados
2. Sweet Corn
3. Pineapples
4. Cabbage
5. Sweet Peas (frozen)
6. Onions
7. Asparagus
8. Mangoes
9. Papayas
10. Kiwi
11. Eggplant
12. Grapefruit
13. Cantaloupe
14. Cauliflower
15. Sweet Potatoes

Top Ten Seasonal Picks

SPRING	SUMMER	AUTUMN	WINTER
Apricot	Bell pepper	Broccoli	Beets
Artichokes	Berries	Brussels S.	B. Endive
Asparagus	Cherries	Cauliflower	Cabbage
Corn	Figs	Collards	Oranges
Grapefruit	Mangos	Cranberries	Kiwi
Green beans	Melons	Grapes	Squash
Leeks	Peaches	Kale	Pears
Rhubarb	S. Squash	Pomegranates	Rutabagas
Spinach	Tomatoes	Pumpkin	Turnips
Strawberries	Zucchini	Swiss Chard	Celery

Five Easy ways to add veggies to things you already make.

1. Ramp up Pasta.

Mix some vegetables into pasta before putting it on your plate. Sometimes when I am pressed for time, I just throw vegetables in the same cooking water as the pasta. Adding chunks of cooked carrots, zucchini, broccoli or cauliflower ramps up the nutritional value of pasta.

Have you ever spiral cut zucchini? It's a wonderful substitution for pasta. So is spaghetti squash.

You can also add pureed carrots and zucchini to marinara or meat sauce for added fiber. Even a picky eater will never know the difference.

2. Soups.

You'll get a whole day's worth of vegetables by blending vegetables into soups. Making your own soups is a great way to take advantage of leftovers too.

4. Sandwich fixings.

Use a wide variety of colorful veggies when constructing sandwiches and burgers. Think outside the box.

5. Pizza.

One of my favorite things to do is to make a rainbow pizza with added toppings of all different colored vegetables, especially green spinach and basil, red tomatoes, yellow peppers or pineapple, black olives and white onions, feta cheese and my favorite brown anchovies.

3. Spreads.

Most of us are familiar with guacamole make from avocados. There are also a ton of vegetables that you can use to make hummus. I make a base of chickpeas (garbanzo beans), tahini (ground sesame seeds), olive oil and garlic. Then I add different flavors to it using a variety of different vegetables and seasonings, such as roasted red peppers.

Basic Hummus

Add some additional seasonings and flavorful veggies, such as red peppers to make a variety of different flavored hummus.

Ingredients:

2 (15 oz.) cans chickpeas (garbanzo beans)
1/4 cup Tahini or ground raw sesame seeds
1 Tbsp. olive oil
1/4 cup lemon juice
1 garlic clove (peeled)
1 tsp. cumin
salt and pepper to taste

Directions:

1. Place all ingredients in high-speed blender.
2. Add extra olive oil or water if needed.

Why do some vegetables stink when you cook them?

Often times it's due to overcooking. But broccoli, cauliflower and all the other members of the cabbage family contain sulfur compounds. When cooked, the particles break down to form other compounds that can smell like rotten eggs. They are not harmful, but the longer the vegetables cooks, the more molecules are released and the stronger the odor becomes.

To reduce odor do this:

To reduce the odor, steam the vegetables only until tender-crisp. Adding a few pieces of bread to the cooking water absorbs the odoriferous compounds. When cooking greens, adding some white vinegar to the boiling water also helps.

Juicing and Blending

I'm often asked if it's better to eat whole fruits and vegetables, juice them in a juicer or use a blender. Basically it all comes down to how fast you want your body to digest the food. In my opinion, I think there are benefits to doing all three.

What's the difference?

Eating whole fruits and vegetables will provide you with so many necessary nutrients. In order for your body to benefit from these nutrients your body must first digest the food.

The more you chew your food, the quicker your digestive system will be able to break the food down so that it can be absorbed into the bloodstream.

Juicing and blending fruits and vegetables also break up the fiber they contain.

Juicing extracts the water and nutrients from fruits and vegetables. In the process juicers discard the fiber. Without the fiber your digestive system doesn't have to work to break the food down.

Blending leaves the fibers in. The more fiber, the longer it will take the digestive process to utilize it.

As a general rule, when you want to get a large amount of nutrients into a person fast, juicing is the quickest way to do so. When you want a more filling nutritious drink, make a smoothie by blending your favorite fruits and vegetables and adding in some yogurt, nuts, seeds and avocado to make it more of a meal.

Making smoothies also allows you to add in other nutrients such as those found in Super foods. Consider adding almond butter or hemp seeds for added protein, Chlorella and Spirulina for added antioxidants and Maca powder to boost the immune system and enhance energy.

There are a ton of different combinations for juicing. I've listed a few below, but before you start juicing there are a few things you need to consider.

While juicing promises incredible benefits, be mindful about giving your body enough time to adjust to becoming healthier.

Also be aware that most fruits and some vegetables can be high in sugar. Juicing lots of apples, carrots and watermelon will make juice taste sweeter, but will also raise your blood sugar very quickly. It's best to only use a small amount of fruit to slightly sweeten your drink if the vegetables you are using aren't quite sweet enough.

When you start loading your body up with a lot of fresh nutrients your body will start eliminating a variety of toxins and waste matter. During this detoxification process you may experience some mild nausea.

Drink your juice slowly to allow your body to make room for these good nutrients.

A couple of wonderful things to add to juice anytime are ginger and lemons.

Ginger has wonderful antioxidant and anti-inflammatory properties.

Lemons help to balance pH levels, improves digestion, cleanses the urinary tract, detoxes the liver and helps strengthen the immune system.

Some juice combinations to get you started:

- Carrots, apple, celery.

- Carrots, beets, ginger.

- Celery, spinach, lemon.

- Kale, spinach, carrots, celery, and ginger.

- Parsley, lettuce, apple and cucumber.

- Wheatgrass, spinach, kale, cucumber, apple, ginger, lime.

What can you do with all the leftover pulp?

There are still a lot of vitamins in the pulp. Add the pulp to meatballs, make some veggie burgers with it, and use it to moisten quick breads, add it to homemade muffins, dips, sauces and soups.

Grains, Nuts, Beans and Seeds

Grains, Nuts, Beans and legumes are the seeds of certain plants. Like all seeds, they contain the potential of a whole new plant. All seeds rely on certain built-in growth inhibitors to keep them from germinating until temperature and moisture conditions are just right. Once sprouting starts, enzyme activity destroys these growth inhibitors and transforms the seed's long-term storage starch into simpler molecules that are easily digested by the growing plant embryo.

Just as the baby plant finds these enzyme-activated molecules easier to digest, so do the people that eat them. So, sprouted grains and legumes are really "live" foods that provide a lot of nutrients that are similar to those found in fresh fruits and vegetables. In fact, when grains are sprouted the starch molecules turn into vegetable sugars. Sprouting also helps make your body absorb calcium, magnesium, iron, copper and zinc and ramp up their protein content.

Seven health benefits of eating sprouted foods:

1. Easier to digest - sprouting breaks down the starches into simple sugars so your body can digest them like a vegetable

2. Lower glycemic index than un-sprouted grains and legumes

3. Increased vitamins B and C, and carotene

4. Increased enzymes

5. Shorter cooking time and can also be eaten raw

6. Reduced anti-nutrients - sprouting neutralizes enzyme inhibitors and phytic acid, a substance present in the bran of all grains, which inhibits absorption of calcium, magnesium, iron, copper and zinc.

7. Sprouts contain a lot of fiber and water and, therefore, are helpful in overcoming constipation.

Chia Seed Overnight Morning Oatmeal

Ingredients:

1/4 cup uncooked old fashioned rolled oats

1/3 cup organic milk or non-dairy milk of your choice

1/4 cup low-fat Greek yogurt

1-1/2 tsp. black or white chia seeds

(White chia seeds can be found at Whole Food market)

2 tsp. maple syrup or honey or stevia (more or less to taste)

1/4 cup blueberries or other fruit combination

1 tsp. vanilla and nutmeg

Directions:

1. In a half pint jar, add oats, milk, yogurt, chia seeds, and maple syrup.
2. Put lid on jar and shake until well combined.
3. Remove lid, add blueberries and stir until mixed throughout.
4. Return lid to jar and refrigerate overnight or up to 2 days.

No need to cook. During the night the oats and chia seeds absorb the liquid and soften. Eat chilled or set out on the counter if you prefer to eat it at room temperature.

Other good flavor combinations: (in place of ¼ cup blueberries) any mixed berries, apple and cinnamon, peanut butter and banana, pineapple coconut, and pumpkin spice.

Tip: For warmer oatmeal, heat some milk in a small saucepan and add the oatmeal. For added crunch, top with chopped almonds or walnuts.

Quick and Easy Flax Seed Muffins

These muffins are great to make in place of eating bed. They come out better in the microwave than they do in the oven.

Chocolate Peanut Butter

Ingredients:

¼ cup of ground flax
1 tsp. baking powder
2 tsp. cocoa powder
2 tsp. peanut or almond butter
1 egg
1 packet of Stevia or 2 tsp. pure maple syrup (my preference)
I've even used a teaspoon of organic strawberry jam or orange marmalade in place of a sweetener.

Directions:

1. Place the ingredients into a mug and put it in the microwave for 50-60 seconds. That's it!

Allow cooling and then enjoying!

I've found that for even cooking, it's important to use a regular shaped square coffee mug.

Alternatively you could make a big batch and bake them in a paper lined muffin pan, but for some reason they just don't rise as well in the oven. If you are against using a microwave you may have better luck than I have. If you come up an oven version, please let me know.

When you make this in a cup in the microwave it makes a huge muffin. I usually divide the ingredients in half and microwave 2 at a time in ramekin cups. That seems to be the perfect amount.

Toppings and other flavors:

I like to top mine with Greek yogurt just before serving.

Basic vanilla.

Omit the cocoa powder and use coconut oil in place of the peanut butter, add in a little vanilla, maybe some cinnamon and microwave. Once cooled, top with your favorite fruit. Fresh berries go good with these vanilla ones.

Carrot cake muffin.

Use basic vanilla recipe. Add finely shredded carrots along with a few walnuts and nutmeg. Top with Greek yogurt and shredded coconut.

Other.

I've also used half flax seeds and half oatmeal to make oatmeal raisin muffin cakes. My grandson loves it when I add chocolate chips to the batter.

You can use almond meal flour in the batter, however I have found that the muffins come out a little dry when I do. Adding pureed fruit seems to help.

Flax Seed Crackers

Ingredients:

2 cups ground flaxseed (I prefer the light golden flax seeds)
1 cup water
1/2 tsp. salt
1/2 tsp. garlic powder
1/2 tsp. onion powder

Directions:

1. Preheat oven to 400 degrees. In a large bowl, combine all the ingredients and mix.

2. Spread evenly onto a parchment or silicone lined baking sheet – about a 1/8 inch thick.

3. Gently cut dough into squares on the baking sheet
(You just need to score the dough so it snaps after it's baked.)
Be careful not to cut up your silicone mat or cookie sheet!)

4. Bake for 20-30 minutes until crisp and edges are browned but not burnt.

Black Bean Brownies

Ingredients:

1 (15.5 ounce) can organic black beans, rinsed and drained
(or 2 cups soft cooked beans)
3 organic eggs
3 Tbsp. liquefied coconut oil
1/4 cup cocoa powder
1 pinch salt
1-tsp. vanilla extract
3/4 cup organic sugar (or sweetener of your choice)
1 tsp. instant coffee
1/2 cup semi-sweet chocolate chips
1/4 cup walnuts

Directions:

Preheat oven to 350 degrees.

1. Lightly grease an 8×8 square baking dish.

2. Combine the black beans, eggs, oil, cocoa powder, salt, vanilla extract, sugar, and instant coffee in a blender and blend until smooth.

4. Pour the liquid mixture into the prepared baking dish. Sprinkle the chocolate chips and walnuts on top of the mixture.

5. Bake in the preheated oven until the top is dry and the edges start to pull away from the sides of the pan, about 30 minutes. Cool 10 minutes before cutting into 16 squares.

Homegrown Sprouting

There are a ton of websites and YouTube videos that contain instructions and charts to teach you how to sprout all kinds of grains and seeds to make micro-greens (tiny plants), or soak to sprout grains, beans and legumes before cooking.

Let me just say, all you have to do to germinate most any grain, bean, legume, nut or seed when you are planning on consuming it within 24 hours is soak it in water overnight. The next day simply pour off and discard the soaking water, give it a quick rinse. From there you can roast (nuts and seeds) or cook (grains, beans and other legumes) as usual.

Tip: Adding a piece of kelp or other seaweed to grains and beans as you cook them adds more minerals to them. I always beans, soak nuts, most seeds, and all grains such as oatmeal the night before. When buying breads and tortillas look for sprouted ones, as they are more nutritious with less of a carbohydrate glycemic load on your system to avoid sugar spikes.

Although there are kits available for sprouting seeds, no special equipment is required. You'll need a clean glass Mason jar, or you can substitute another wide-mouth glass jar. Use cheesecloth, a stainless steel metal screen or even old (clean) pantyhose to cover the mouth of the jar, and secure the covering with a ring lid, rubber band, or string.

Most people are familiar with the long, thick mung bean sprouts that are often served with Chow Mein. You can easily grow these and similar sturdy sprouts using dried mung beans, dried peas, lentils and soybeans in a mason jar at home.

Smaller tiny leaf sprouts found in the produce section of most grocery stores are radish sprouts, clover sprouts, broccoli sprouts and alfalfa sprouts. Although the process is the same for sprouting these delicate plants it's important to be cautious when growing these sprouts at home due to the possibility of mold forming if you are not able to drain them well enough due to the seed's tiny size. If you like to juice, you may want to try growing your own wheatgrass too.

How to Sprout in a Mason Jar

I've chosen lentils as an example here as lentils are one of the easiest to sprout.

What you will need:

1/2 cup dried lentils (or use mung, peas, or soybeans)
water
quart jar
small piece of cheesecloth
mason jar band or rubber band

Directions:

1. Pour lentils into the quart jar and rinse using lukewarm water. I just use my hand to cover the top of the jar and let the water run out through my fingers while holding the lentils inside.

3. Once lentils are rinsed add just enough water to cover the top of the lentils by about an inch.

4. Place cheesecloth on top of the jar and secure it down with a Mason jar band or a rubber band.

5. Keep the jar (upright) in a warm, dark place overnight. A kitchen cabinet works well.

6. Take out the jar and drain the soak water (again, I just take the cheesecloth/band off and drain it out through my hand).

7. Fill the jar with fresh, lukewarm water to rinse and then drain all the water out.

8. Replace the cheesecloth/band and return the jar to the warm, dark location, this time setting the jar on its side or upside down at about a 45 degree angle to help with drainage. Put the jar in a shallow dish for water to drain into.

9. Take the jar out once or twice a day to rinse the contents.

10. Depending on how warm your house is, within one to three days, you'll see the first tiny shoots coming forth.

By day five or within about a week the jar will be full of lentil sprouts measuring an inch or so long. This is the perfect time to eat them.

How to use: Eat raw as a snack (they're delicious!) or add them to salads. Mix them in a stir-fry with seasonings or use them in sandwiches in place of lettuce. To store, keep them in the fridge. You can store your sprouts in the same jar you used for sprouting.

Cultured Foods

Cultured foods; often referred to as fermented or probiotic foods, help to boost good gut bacteria and improve digestive, cardiovascular and immune health.

The fermentation process preserves the food and creates lactic acid, enzymes, vitamins, omega-3 fatty acids and probiotics that make the food more digestible.

Three top probiotic foods are:
1. Yogurt,
2. Kefir
3. Sauerkraut.

Tip: Eat a small amount of cultured vegetables with every meal to improve your digestive and gut flora (necessary good bacteria).

One of the easiest to make is sauerkraut (made from raw cabbage). Almost any vegetable can be cultured.

Homemade (Fermented Cabbage) Sauerkraut

Basic Recipe 1
1 heads green cabbage, shredded
(The finer you shred the cabbage the quicker it will ferment.)
1 Tbsp. sea salt

Fermentation Directions:

1. Place shredded cabbage in a large bowl.

2. Add 1 Tablespoon of sea salt for every head of cabbage you use to make a brine. Sea salt helps to release water from the cellular walls of the cabbage.

3. To help it along, massage the cabbage with your hands.

4. Pack mixture (cabbage and brine) down into a glass or ceramic, airtight, container. Use your fist, a wooden dowel, or a potato masher to pack veggies tightly.

5. Fill container almost full, but leave about 2 inches of room at the top for veggies to expand. Make sure cabbage is covered with brine or add extra water.

6. Place several cabbage leaves on top to fill the remaining 2-inch space. Clamp jar closed.

7. Let veggies sit out at room temperature (70-degrees) for at least five days. Ten days is even better. Place a plate underneath to catch any leaking liquid.

During the fermentation period, the friendly bacteria are reproducing and converting the sugars and starches to lactic acid. Once the initial process is over, it is time to slow down the bacterial activity by putting the cultured vegetables in the refrigerator. The cold will greatly slow the fermentation, but does not stop it completely, even if the veggies sit in your refrigerator for months. Almost any vegetable can be fermented. The directions are the same.

Here are a few more combinations to try:
Use same fermentation directions for both.

Recipe 2
1 head red cabbage, shredded
2 large carrots, shredded
1-inch piece of ginger, peeled and chopped
2 cloves garlic, peeled and chopped
1 Tbsp. sea salt

Recipe 3 (triple recipe)
3 heads green cabbage, shredded
2 bunch kale, chopped
2 garlic clove, whole
2 cups wakame or other soaked and chopped seaweed
(measured after soaking)
3 Tbsp. of sea salt (1 Tbsp. per head of cabbage)

Prebiotics, Probiotics, Antibiotics

What's the difference?

Prebiotics act as food for probiotics. Prebiotics are found in such things as whole grains, onions and garlic.

Probiotics are "live microorganisms found in such foods as fermented dairy products, such as yogurt and kefir and cultured vegetables such as sauerkraut, Kim chi, and pickled vegetables.

When prebiotics and probiotics are combined, they are considered symbiotic because they contain live bacteria and the fuel they need to thrive.

Bacteria? Why would you want to consume anything that has live bacteria in it? It's all about balance. Our digestive system normally has both "good" bacteria and "bad" bacteria. Maintaining the correct balance between the "good" bacteria and the "bad" bacteria is necessary for optimal health.

Things like medications, diet, diseases, and our environment can upset that balance.

Antibiotics are a major culprit in upsetting that balance.
Antibiotics are designed to do kill bacteria. It does a good job of doing so, but the side affect is that it kills both good and bad bacteria. So you need to replenish your supply. The best way is by eating probiotics.

Greek Yogurt Cheesecake

For graham cracker crust:

1/2 cup melted butter
1 ½ cups graham cracker crumbs
2 Tbsp. sugar
1/8 tsp. salt

Directions:

1. Mix all ingredients together.

2. Press into bottom of pie pan and set aside.
   (I like making individual ones in Ramekin cups)

For Cheesecake filling:

2 cups thick Greek yogurt
(To thicken yogurt strain it through a cheesecloth to remove more of the whey.)
2 eggs
½ cup sugar
1 tsp. vanilla
1 Tbsp. cornstarch
pinch of salt

Directions:

Preheat oven to 350 degrees
1. Mix all ingredients EXCEPT the cornstarch and salt until smooth. This can be done whisking by hand or in a blender.

2. Add the cornstarch and salt. Mix well.

3. Pour mixture into a graham cracker crust.
Sometimes I don't even use the graham cracker crust.

4. Bake for 35 to 40 minutes or until the center jiggles when the pan is gently shaken but the edges of the cheesecake are set.

I usually make my own yogurt, draining a lot of the whey from it for a very thick and rich tasting cheesecake. To get similar results from store bought yogurt, simply let the yogurt whey drain through a piece of cheesecloth in the refrigerator overnight.

Non-Dairy Milks and Cream

Raw nut milks are rich in vitamins, minerals and nutrients. Unlike store bought, when you make it yourself, you know you have 100% pure, raw almond milk without any additives, preservatives, or chemicals! (For instance store bought almond milk is made from a combination of pasteurized almonds, sugar, water, emulsifiers, and stabilizers.)

Tip: Since homemade milk is preservative free, it must be refrigerated immediately after blending and should be consumed within 24 hours.

For each of these recipes, blend all ingredients together in a high-speed blender. After blending if the milk tastes too grainy you can always strain away the pulp. Refrigerate. Shake well before serving.

Almond Milk
1 cup raw almonds*
3 cups water
sweetener to taste (optional)
1 tsp. vanilla (optional)

Strain the pulp if desired. To easily adjust milk consistency, add or decrease the amount of water you use.
* You will get a whiter, less grainy milk remove the skins first, by soaking or blanching the almonds ahead of time, which makes it easy to remove the skins.

In a hurry?
Make this quick almond milk using almond butter.

QUICK Almond Milk
1 cup Almond Milk
Stir 2 – 3 tsp. of almond butter
into 1 cup water

Hemp Milk
1 cup hulled hemp seeds
5 cups water

Coconut Milk
1 cup shredded fresh coconut meat
2 cups water

Rice Milk
½ cup cooked brown rice
2 cups water
1 tsp. vanilla
sweetener to taste (optional)

Mocha Almond Milk Shake

Ingredients:

1 cup non-dairy almond milk
1 Tbsp. white chocolate chips
(milk chocolate chips are good too)
1 tsp. instant coffee
1 tsp. vanilla

sweeten to taste
1/2 cup crushed ice

Directions:

Place all in a high-speed blender and mix until smooth.

Cashew Cream

Cashew cream is a great substitute for a non-dairy whipped cream topping. The following recipe makes 3 cups, which will keep in the refrigerator for up to one week.

Ingredients:

2 cups raw cashews
8 cups boiling water

Directions:

1. Cover 2 cups raw cashews with 8 cups boiling water in large bowl.

2. Cover with a clean kitchen towel, and let stand 6 to 8 hours.

3. Drain cashews, and then blend in blender with 1/3 to 1/2 cup cold water until smooth and thick.

My Moto:

"Attitude Is So Important!"

About the Author

Elaine Lombardi is married 43 years, the mother of 4 adult-children, and a devoted grandmother. Her career background has been in Early Childhood Education as a former preschool director and teacher and is currently a board Certified Holistic Health Coach. She also holds certifications in the fields of physical fitness, aquatics and holistic modalities, such as EFT, Reiki and Reflexology.

Lombardi is passionate about the work she does. Whether she is working one on one with an individual client, counseling a family as a whole, presenting a program to a group, or lecturing to the public, the work she does always centers around encouraging possibilities.

Elaine enjoys gardening, cooking and teaching what she knows about food, nutrition, personal care and wellness practices. She developed The H.E.A.L. Approach to health and wellness and creates completely personalized "roadmap to health" programs to suit individual's unique body and lifestyle preferences.

Elaine is a public speaker and educates people at health conferences and events around the country. She also teaches workshops at corporate wellness "lunch and learn" training sessions. She offers both private and group health coaching sessions to men, women and children of all ages. She loves working with individuals who want to lose weight, rid their body of debilitating inflammation, reclaim their health and live a more vibrant, energetic, productive life.

Elaine writes informative articles and facilitates an online support blog for caregivers at www.HealthCoachForCaregivers.com.

She resides with her husband in Laguna Woods, California. To contact Elaine Lombardi visit her website www.ElaineLombardi.com or email her at Elaine@ElaineLombardi.com.

Made in the USA
Charleston, SC
12 April 2015